365 LESSONS FROM THE

STOICS

COMPILED BY ANDREA KIRK ASSAF

William Collins
an imprint of HarperCollins*Publishers*
1 London Bridge Street
London SE1 9GF

WilliamCollinsBooks.com

HarperCollins*Publishers*
Macken House, 39/40 Mayor Street Upper,
Dublin 1, D01 C9W8, Ireland

First published by HarperCollins*Publishers* in 2024

1 3 5 7 9 10 8 6 4 2

Compiled by Andrea Kirk Assaf
Cover and interior page design by e-Digital Design Ltd
Senior editor: Simon Holland

Andrea Kirk Assaf asserts the moral right to be identified
as the compiler of this work.

A catalogue record for this book is available from the British Library.

ISBN: 978-0-00-871415-4

Printed and bound in Bosnia

365 LESSONS FROM THE
STOICS

Transform your Daily Life

Using the Stoics' Wisdom

and Understanding

WITH QUOTES FROM SENECA, EPICTETUS AND MARCUS AURELIUS

COMPILED BY ANDREA KIRK ASSAF

WILLIAM
COLLINS

I dedicate this book to the memory of my father, Russell Amos Kirk, who introduced me to Stoicism through both word and example.

He kept his Stoic principles close throughout his life, tempered by Christian hope.

CONTENTS

HOW TO USE THIS BOOK

What would a Stoic's day look like? And how could this small, portable book of Stoic quotes be a useful companion through it? A Stoic's day is marked by mindfulness, discipline and reflection. This collection of Stoic quotes aims to be your companion through it all. With this volume on the nightstand, you can start your day by recalling the words of Marcus Aurelius, perhaps the most famous of all Stoics. He wrote this dialogue with himself while residing in a military camp by the Danube river.

"In the morning when thou risest unwillingly, let this thought be present – I am rising to the work of a human being. Why then am I dissatisfied if I am going to do the things for which I exist and for which I was brought into the world? Or have I been made for this, to lie in the bed-clothes and keep myself warm? But this is more pleasant. Dost thou exist then to take thy pleasure, and not at all for action or exertion? Dost thou not see the little plants, the little birds, the ants, the spiders, the bees working together to put in order their several parts of the universe? And art thou unwilling to do the work of a human being, and dost thou not make haste to do that which is according to thy nature?"

Once the feet have touched the ground and the challenge of life has been accepted, it is the ideal time to make a statement of affirmation and gratitude. In Aurelius' words: *"When you arise in the morning, think of what a precious privilege it is to be alive – to breathe, to think, to enjoy, to love."*

As the Stoic embarks upon the day, fraught with opportunities to grow in virtue through exercising one's 'ruling principle', it might help every now and then to take this book out of the bag or the desk drawer, to give oneself a reality check in order to mentally prepare for the worst-case scenario. Or, as our philosopher-king put it:

"…tell yourself: the people I deal with today will be meddling, ungrateful, arrogant, dishonest, jealous and surly. They are like this because they can't tell good from evil. But I have seen the beauty of good, and the ugliness of evil, and have recognized that the wrongdoer has a nature related to my own – not of the same blood and birth, but the same mind, and possessing a share of the divine. And so none of them can hurt me. No one can implicate me in ugliness. Nor can I feel angry at my relative, or hate him. We were born to work together like feet, hands and eyes, like the two rows of teeth, upper and lower. To obstruct each other is unnatural. To feel anger at someone, to turn your back on him: these are unnatural."

At nightfall, one can again imitate the example of Marcus, who nightly withdrew into his own mind and reflected upon all that had transpired, often through writing in his diary. Placing a journal next to this book, or even scribbling in the book itself, would encourage the adoption of another crucial Stoic habit – an end-of-the-day personal review through journalling.

As the eyelids close, one can retain these beautiful and heartening words of Seneca:

"Let us go to our sleep with joy and gladness; let us say: I have lived; And if God is pleased to add another day, we should welcome it with glad hearts. When a man has said: 'I have lived!', every morning he arises he receives a bonus."

Memento Mori, remember your death, is perhaps the most well known of the Stoic sayings, and this nightly reflection reminds us that each day is a life unto itself and that tomorrow is not guaranteed. As Seneca says: *"…one day, mind you, is a stage on life's journey."*

Supporting your day with these Stoic sayings, as bookends from dawn to dark, may you find this little book to be a trusted companion on your own life journey.

INTRODUCTION TO THE STOICS AND STOICISM

Wisdom. Courage. Justice. Temperance. These are what are known as the four Stoic virtues that students of the philosophy strive to cultivate through reading, reasoning, dialogue and habitual practices. The value of these virtues, one could argue, is that they all assist in the attainment of another very practical virtue that is in great demand today – resilience.

The Stoics were realists who taught that most circumstances in life are beyond our control, a truth many of the younger generations have been confronted with since the Covid-19 lockdown deprived them of many personal freedoms they had taken for granted. Unlike the 'greatest generation', who were taught resilience through the harrowing experiences and hardships of World War II, the generations since have lived – at least in the Western world – in relative security. And so, when disaster strikes and foundations are shaken, as inevitably occurs, the perennial wisdom of the Stoics resurfaces and is given fresh relevance.

We are in a moment such as this. You may find, as you dip into these pages, that the three voices in this book, though their bones turned to dust two millennia ago, sound as if they are speaking directly to your daily struggles. This is no accident, for each author confronted the same realities of human nature that we do today – from resisting the temptation to stay in a warm, comfortable bed in the morning, to tempering anger in the face of injustices or disappointments throughout the day, to night-time sleepless enslavement to fears and anxieties regarding the future.

These things said, Stoicism provides more than wise words to turn to in times of crisis. It offers a deeply formative method for character development through practices that modern-day readers will be familiar with – mindfulness, gratitude, intentionality, affirmation, introspection, habit-building, emotional regulation and magnanimity. The Stoic is not born equipped with these superpowers; such capabilities are cultivated through trial and error, one moment at a time, fostering resilience.

> *"When force of circumstance upsets your equanimity, lose no time in recovering your self-control, and do not remain out of tune longer than you can help. Habitual recurrence to the harmony will increase your mastery of it."* – Marcus Aurelius

Stoicism is a philosophy of action, not just theory. It exists, as all philosophies do, for the purpose of providing reasoned principles to serve as guides in the formation of mindset, moral action and *eudaimonia* – translated as 'human flourishing', or 'a well-lived life'. The three thinkers presented here are representative of Stoic philosophy in general, which accounts for their name recognition, and the three works selected are, in turn, representative of their thought. Allow me to present them to you in the context of their Stoic lineage.

It all began with a storm at sea in the third century BCE. A successful merchant of the highly prized Tyrian dye lost his ship and his entire fortune with it, washing ashore penniless in Greece. Zeno of Citium, as he was known, turned to the consolation of philosophy in Athens – first studying under Crates of Thebes, the founder of the Cynic school, before founding his own school. Zeno's students gathered on a painted porch in the Agora – the *stoa poikilê* – and came to be called Stoics.

Each of Zeno's successors left his own mark on Stoicism – Cleanthes, Chrysippus, Zeno of Tarsus, Diogenes of Babylon, Antipater of Tarsus and Panaetius of Rhodes. Stoicism spread to Rome and was championed by such diverse individuals as Roman statesmen Cato the Younger and Seneca the Younger, the freed Greek slave Epictetus (as recorded by his student Arrian), and, most famously, the emperor of the Roman empire himself, Marcus Aurelius.

With the fall of the Roman Empire, over two hundred years would pass before Stoicism was rediscovered and appreciated by great Christian minds such as St. Ambrose, St. Augustine, St. Jerome and Boethius. Stoicism's next dusting-off and repolishing came about thanks to the Flemish Renaissance humanist Justus Lipsius, who led a philosophical movement in the late sixteenth century that combined Stoic virtues with Christian beliefs. Lipsius promoted Stoicism in part as a response to the religious wars of the day, and it was during this time that Stoicism was referred to as a 'crisis philosophy', with Lipsius advocating the virtue of 'constancy' in the face of political and religious upheaval.

Although Stoic physics and logic were largely abandoned, their virtue ethics continued to shape philosophy and theology – notably in the work of René Descartes, Benedict de Spinoza and Blaise Pascal – up to today. In the twentieth century, with the development of rational emotive behaviour therapy by Albert Ellis, and then cognitive behavioural therapy by Aaron T. Beck, Stoicism found a partner in modern scientific inquiry and application. The twenty-first century has seen such a resurgence of interest in the philosophy, particularly in the last few years since the pandemic, that it has been given a new name – Modern Stoicism – with a focus on harnessing the ability of Stoic principles and practices for the prevention of potential mental health issues surrounding trauma and stress.

Returning to the three Stoic authors of ancient Rome featured in these pages, let us understand the complex realities each one lived through, which led them to write these words that we can now read today for our own benefit.

Lucius Annaeus Seneca, also known as Seneca the Younger, was a Roman statesman, orator, playwright – and, of course, Stoic philosopher. Living between 4 BCE and 65 CE, Seneca had the misfortune to be a leading intellectual figure during the reign of emperors Caligula, who nearly killed him, Claudius, who sent him into exile, and then Nero, who ordered him to commit suicide. In between these tragedies, Seneca was a powerful quaestor, private tutor to the future emperor Nero, and de facto co-ruler of Rome during the early years of Nero's reign. Withdrawing from political intrigue in his final years of retirement, he authored the majority of his Stoic work, including the 124 letters to his younger friend Lucilius, full of personal anecdotes, observations and advice, particularly about the beauty and wisdom of cooperating with nature.

Epictetus lived in Rome during the last decades of Seneca's life and would certainly be aware of the famous statesman's career, writings and demise, though Epictetus was in a very different social class. Born as a Greek slave in Phrygia, Epictetus lived most of his life in Rome as the property of Nero's secretary, Epaphroditus. A gifted intellect, Epictetus was sent to study under the Stoic philosopher Musonius Rufus. Following the death of Nero and then his master, Epictetus obtained his freedom and began teaching philosophy in Rome, only to be banished by the emperor Domitian in 93 CE, along with all philosophers. The remaining years of his long life were spent teaching at a school he founded in Greece, where his pupil Arrian recorded his wisdom in *The Discourses and The Enchiridion*, or Handbook. He urged his students, in his sarcastic and reprimanding style, to recall that Stoicism is a way of life – *modus vivendi* – not mere theory. External events are beyond our control, Epictetus explains, but we can control our reactions to them, through consistent self-discipline.

Marcus Aurelius is history's most unlikely example of a Stoic. From childhood he demonstrated a virtuous character, and even during his lifetime he was known as the philosopher-king, that rare combination of a man of both contemplation and action. Marcus Aurelius Antoninus became heir to the Nerva-Antonine dynasty through adoption and was groomed to rule. He was also educated for wisdom and was well read in the Stoic tradition, including the works of Epictetus. Our modern concept of Stoicism largely comes from Marcus' private writings, never intended for publication, but nevertheless widely read ever since its public appearance in 180 CE. In *Meditations* we encounter a figure who continually took recourse to the consolation of philosophy as he faced one war after another, a plague of historic proportions, and the deaths of seven of his children. Marcus' continual reminder to himself was about the brevity of life, and the rewards of living it virtuously. Or, as he so succinctly puts it: *"Do not act as if thou wert going to live ten thousand years. Death hangs over thee. While thou livest, while it is in thy power, be good."*

Finally, let's conclude by again heeding the exhortation of this resilient philosopher-king, who spent approximately nineteen years giving himself the following advice in his diary: *"No longer talk at all about the kind of man that a good man ought to be, but be such."*

Andrea Kirk Assaf
May, 2024
Rome, Italy

365 LESSONS

VIRTUE

God has not only given us these faculties, by which we shall be able to bear everything that happens without being depressed or broken by it; but, like a good king and a true father, He has given us these faculties free from hindrance, subject to no compulsion, unimpeded, and has put them entirely in our own power, without even having reserved to Himself any power of hindering or impeding. You, who have received these powers free and as your own, use them not; you do not even see what you have received, and from whom; some of you being blinded to the giver, and not even acknowledging your benefactor, and others, through meanness of spirit, betaking yourselves to fault-finding and making charges against God. Yet I will show to you that you have powers and means for greatness of soul and manliness; but what powers you have for finding fault and making accusations, do you show me.

EPICTETUS, *THE TEACHINGS OF A STOIC:
SELECTED DISCOURSES AND THE ENCHIRIDION,*
"OF PROVIDENCE" (FROM C. EARLY 2ND CENTURY CE)

ACCEPTANCE

Every moment think steadily as a Roman and a man to do what thou hast in hand with perfect and simple dignity, and feeling of affection, and freedom, and justice; and to give thyself relief from all other thoughts. And thou wilt give thyself relief, if thou doest every act of thy life as if it were the last, laying aside all carelessness and passionate aversion from the commands of reason, and all hypocrisy, and self-love, and discontent with the portion which has been given to thee.

MARCUS AURELIUS, *MEDITATIONS*, "BOOK II" (FROM C. 180 CE)

VIRTUE

So let us also win the way to victory in all our struggles – for the reward is not a garland or a palm or a trumpeter who calls for silence at the proclamation of our names, but rather virtue, steadfastness of soul, and a peace that is won for all time, if fortune has once been utterly vanquished in any combat.

LUCIUS SENECA, *LETTERS FROM A STOIC*, "LXXVIII. ON THE HEALING POWER OF THE MIND" (FROM C. 63-65 CE)

TIME

4

Do not act as if thou wert going to live ten thousand years. Death hangs over thee. While thou livest, while it is in thy power, be good.

MARCUS AURELIUS, *MEDITATIONS*, "BOOK IV" (FROM C. 180 CE)

DETACHMENT

5

Remember that desire contains in it the profession (hope) of obtaining that which you desire; and the profession (hope) in aversion (turning from a thing) is that you will not fall into that which you attempt to avoid; and he who fails in his desire is unfortunate; and he who falls into that which he would avoid is unhappy. If then you attempt to avoid only the things contrary to nature which are within your power you will not be involved in any of the things which you would avoid. But if you attempt to avoid disease, or death, or poverty, you will be unhappy. Take away then aversion from all things which are not in our power, and transfer it to the things contrary to nature which are in our power.

EPICTETUS, *THE TEACHINGS OF A STOIC: SELECTED DISCOURSES AND THE ENCHIRIDION*, "THE MANUAL: II" (FROM C. EARLY 2ND CENTURY CE)

DETACHMENT

6

Where is the nature of evil and good? It is where truth is: where truth is and where nature is, there is caution: where truth is, there is courage where nature is. For this reason also it is ridiculous to say, Suggest something to me (tell me what to do). What should I suggest to you? Well, form my mind so as to accommodate itself to any event. Why that is just the same as if a man who is ignorant of letters should say, Tell me what to write when any name is proposed to me… But if you have practised writing, you are also prepared to write (or to do) anything that is required. If you are not, what can I now suggest? For if circumstances require something else, what will you say, or what will you do? Remember then this general precept and you will need no suggestion. But if you gape after externals, you must of necessity ramble up and down in obedience to the will of your master. And who is the master? He who has the power over the things which you seek to gain or try to avoid.

EPICTETUS, *THE TEACHINGS OF A STOIC:*
SELECTED DISCOURSES AND THE ENCHIRIDION,
"OF TRANQUILITY (FREEDOM FROM PERTURBATION)"
(FROM C. EARLY 2ND CENTURY CE)

GOODNESS

The agent is God; the source, matter; the form, the shape and the arrangement of the visible world. The pattern is doubtless the model according to which God has made this great and most beautiful creation. The purpose is his object in so doing. Do you ask what God's purpose is? It is goodness. Plato, at any rate, says: "What was God's reason for creating the world? God is good, and no good person is grudging of anything that is good. Therefore, God made it the best world possible."

LUCIUS SENECA, *LETTERS FROM A STOIC*, "LXV. ON THE FIRST CAUSE" (FROM C. 63-65 CE)

WISDOM

I shall keep watching myself continually, and – a most useful habit – shall review each day. For this is what makes us wicked: that no one of us looks back over his own life. Our thoughts are devoted only to what we are about to do. And yet our plans for the future always depend on the past.

LUCIUS SENECA, *LETTERS FROM A STOIC*, "LXXVIII. ON THE HEALING POWER OF THE MIND" (FROM C. 63-65 CE)

COOPERATION WITH NATURE

Begin the morning by saying to thyself, I shall meet with the busybody, the ungrateful, arrogant, deceitful, envious, unsocial. All these things happen to them by reason of their ignorance of what is good and evil. But I who have seen the nature of the good that it is beautiful, and of the bad that it is ugly, and the nature of him who does wrong, that it is akin to me, not only of the same blood or seed, but that it participates in the same intelligence and the same portion of the divinity, I can neither be injured by any of them, for no one can fix on me what is ugly, nor can I be angry with my kinsman, nor hate him. For we are made for cooperation, like feet, like hands, like eyelids, like the rows of the upper and lower teeth. To act against one another then is contrary to nature; and it is acting against one another to be vexed and to turn away.

MARCUS AURELIUS, *MEDITATIONS*, "BOOK II" (FROM C. 180 CE)

VIRTUE

The best way of avenging thyself is not to become like the wrongdoer.

MARCUS AURELIUS, *MEDITATIONS*, "BOOK VI" (FROM C. 180 CE)

VIRTUE

11

He who is making progress, having learned from philosophers that desire means the desire of good things, and aversion means aversion from bad things; having learned too that happiness and tranquillity are not attainable by man otherwise than by not failing to obtain what he desires, and not falling into that which he would avoid; such a man takes from himself desire altogether and confers it, but he employs his aversion only on things which are dependent on his will. For if he attempts to avoid anything independent of his will, he knows that sometimes he will fall in with something which he wishes to avoid, and he will be unhappy. Now if virtue promises good fortune and tranquillity and happiness, certainly also the progress towards virtue is progress towards each of these things. For it is always true that to whatever point the perfecting of anything leads us, progress is an approach towards this point.

EPICTETUS, *THE TEACHINGS OF A STOIC: SELECTED DISCOURSES AND THE ENCHIRIDION*, "OF PROGRESS OR IMPROVEMENT" (FROM C. EARLY 2ND CENTURY CE)

VIRTUE

12

Ponder for a long time whether you shall admit a given person to your friendship; but when you have decided to admit him, welcome him with all your heart and soul. Speak as boldly with him as with yourself. As to yourself, although you should live in such a way that you trust your own self with nothing which you could not entrust even to your enemy, yet, since certain matters occur which convention keeps secret, you should share with a friend at least all your worries and reflections. Regard him as loyal, and you will make him loyal.

LUCIUS SENECA, *THE EPISTLES OF SENECA, III.*
"ON TRUE AND FALSE FRIENDSHIP" (APPROX. 62 CE)

WISDOM

13

Philosophy does not propose to secure for a man any external thing. If it did (or if it were not, as I say), philosophy would be allowing some thing which is not within its province. For as the carpenter's material is wood, and that of the statuary is copper, so the matter of the art of living is each man's life.

EPICTETUS, *THE TEACHINGS OF A STOIC: SELECTED DISCOURSES AND THE ENCHIRIDION,* "WHAT PHILOSOPHY PROMISES" (FROM C. EARLY 2ND CENTURY CE)

GOODNESS

14

From everything, which is or happens in the world, it is easy to praise Providence, if a man possesses these two qualities: the faculty of seeing what belongs and happens to all persons and things, and a grateful disposition. If he does not possess these two qualities, one man will not see the use of things which are and which happen: another will not be thankful for them, even if he does know them.

EPICTETUS, *THE TEACHINGS OF A STOIC:*
SELECTED DISCOURSES AND THE ENCHIRIDION,
"OF PROVIDENCE" (FROM C. EARLY 2ND CENTURY CE)

COOPERATION WITH NATURE

15

Food does no good and is not assimilated into the body if it leaves the stomach as soon as it is eaten; nothing hinders a cure so much as frequent change of medicine; no wound will heal when one salve is tried after another; a plant which is often moved can never grow strong. There is nothing so efficacious that it can be helpful while it is being shifted about.

LUCIUS SENECA, *LETTERS FROM A STOIC*, "II. ON
DISCURSIVENESS IN READING" (FROM C. 63-65 CE)

WISDOM

…let us go to our sleep with joy and gladness; let us say: I have lived; the course which Fortune set for me is finished. And if God is pleased to add another day, we should welcome it with glad hearts. That man is happiest, and is secure in his own possession of himself, who can await the morrow without apprehension. When a man has said: "I have lived!", every morning he arises he receives a bonus.

LUCIUS SENECA, *LETTERS FROM A STOIC*, "XII. ON OLD AGE"
(FROM C. 63-65 CE)

ACCEPTANCE

Be like the promontory against which the waves continually break, but it stands firm and tames the fury of the water around it. Unhappy am I because this has happened to me? Not so, but happy am I, though this has happened to me, because I continue free from pain, neither crushed by the present nor fearing the future. For such a thing as this might have happened to every man; but every man would not have continued free from pain on such an occasion.

MARCUS AURELIUS, *MEDITATIONS*, "BOOK IV" (FROM C. 180 CE)

ACCEPTANCE

18

If you would have your children and your wife and your friends to live forever, you are silly; for you would have the things which are not in your power to be in your power, and the things which belong to others to be yours… He is the master of every man who has the power over the things which another person wishes or does not wish, the power to confer them on him or to take them away. Whoever then wishes to be free let him neither wish for anything nor avoid anything which depends on others: if he does not observe this rule, he must be a slave.

EPICTETUS, *THE TEACHINGS OF A STOIC: SELECTED DISCOURSES AND THE ENCHIRIDION*, "THE MANUAL: XIV" (FROM C. EARLY 2ND CENTURY CE)

DETACHMENT

19

I can have that opinion about anything, which I ought to have. If I can, why am I disturbed? The things which are external to my mind have no relation at all to my mind. Let this be the state of thy affects, and thou standest erect. To recover thy life is in thy power. Look at things again as thou didst use to look at them; for in this consists the recovery of thy life.

MARCUS AURELIUS, *MEDITATIONS*, "BOOK VII" (FROM C. 180 CE)

NOBILITY OF THOUGHT

I commend you and rejoice in the fact that you are persistent in your studies, and that, putting all else aside, you make it each day your endeavour to become a better man. I do not merely exhort you to keep at it; I actually beg you to do so. I warn you, however, not to act after the fashion of those who desire to be conspicuous rather than to improve, by doing things which will rouse comment as regards your dress or general way of living. Repellent attire, unkempt hair, slovenly beard, open scorn of silver dishes, a couch on the bare earth, and any other perverted forms of self-display, are to be avoided... Inwardly, we ought to be different in all respects, but our exterior should conform to society... Let us try to maintain a higher standard of life than that of the multitude, but not a contrary standard; otherwise, we shall frighten away and repel the very persons whom we are trying to improve.

LUCIUS SENECA, *LETTERS FROM A STOIC*, "V. ON THE PHILOSOPHER'S MEAN" (FROM C. 63-65 CE)

The wise and good man then, after considering all these things, submits his own mind to him who administers the whole, as good citizens do to the law of the state. He who is receiving instruction ought to come to be instructed with this intention. How shall I follow the gods in all things, how shall I be contented with the divine administration, and how can I become free? For he is free to whom everything happens according to his will, and whom no man can hinder. What then, is freedom madness? Certainly not; for madness and freedom do not consist. But, you say, I would have everything result just as I like, and in whatever way I like. You are mad, you are beside yourself. Do you not know that freedom is a noble and valuable thing? But for me inconsiderately to wish for things to happen as I inconsiderately like, this appears to be not only not noble, but even most base.

EPICTETUS, *THE TEACHINGS OF A STOIC: SELECTED DISCOURSES AND THE ENCHIRIDION*, "OF CONTENTMENT" (FROM C. EARLY 2ND CENTURY CE)

COOPERATION WITH NATURE

For love of bustle is not industry – it is only the restlessness of a hunted mind. And true repose does not consist in condemning all motion as merely vexation; that kind of repose is slackness and inertia. Therefore, you should note the following saying, taken from my reading in Pomponius: "Some men shrink into dark corners, to such a degree that they see darkly by day." No, men should combine these tendencies, and he who reposes should act and he who acts should take repose. Discuss the problem with Nature; she will tell you that she has created both day and night.

LUCIUS SENECA, *LETTERS FROM A STOIC*, "III. ON TRUE AND FALSE FRIENDSHIP" (FROM C. 63-65 CE)

WILL

Nature gave us legs with which to do our own walking, and eyes with which to do our own seeing. Our luxuries have condemned us to weakness; we have ceased to be able to do that which we have long declined to do.

LUCIUS SENECA, *LETTERS FROM A STOIC*, "LV. ON VATIA'S VILLA" (FROM C. 63-65 CE)

WILL

24

Do the things external which fall upon thee distract thee?
Give thyself time to learn something new and good, and
cease to be whirled around. But then thou must also avoid
being carried about the other way. For those too are triflers
who have wearied themselves in life by their activity, and yet
have no object to which to direct every movement, and, in
a word, all their thoughts.

MARCUS AURELIUS, *MEDITATIONS*, "BOOK II" (FROM C. 180 CE)

WISDOM

25

Accordingly, since you cannot read all the books which you
may possess, it is enough to possess only as many books as
you can read. "But," you reply, "I wish to dip first into one
book and then into another." I tell you that it is the sign
of an overnice appetite to toy with many dishes; for when
they are manifold and varied, they cloy but do not nourish.
So you should always read standard authors; and when you
crave a change, fall back upon those whom you read before.

LUCIUS SENECA, *LETTERS FROM A STOIC*, "II.
ON DISCURSIVENESS IN READING" (FROM C. 63-65 CE)

COOPERATION WITH NATURE

Thou must now at last perceive of what universe thou art a part, and of what administrator of the universe thy existence is an efflux, and that a limit of time is fixed for thee, which if thou dost not use for clearing away the clouds from thy mind, it will go and thou wilt go, and it will never return.

MARCUS AURELIUS, *MEDITATIONS*, "BOOK II" (FROM C. 180 CE)

WISDOM

...no man can live a happy life, or even a supportable life, without the study of wisdom; you know also that a happy life is reached when our wisdom is brought to completion, but that life is at least endurable even when our wisdom is only begun. This idea, however, clear though it is, must be strengthened and implanted more deeply by daily reflection; it is more important for you to keep the resolutions you have already made than to go on and make noble ones. You must persevere, must develop new strength by continuous study, until that which is only a good inclination becomes a good settled purpose.

LUCIUS SENECA, *LETTERS FROM A STOIC*, "XVI. ON PHILOSOPHY, THE GUIDE OF LIFE" (FROM C. 63-65 CE)

COOPERATION WITH NATURE

28

Through not observing what is in the mind of another a man has seldom been seen to be unhappy; but those who do not observe the movements of their own minds must of necessity be unhappy. This thou must always bear in mind, what is the nature of the whole, and what is my nature, and how this is related to that, and what kind of a part it is of what kind of a whole; and that there is no one who hinders thee from always doing and saying the things which are according to the nature of which thou art a part.

MARCUS AURELIUS, *MEDITATIONS*, "BOOK II" (FROM C. 180 CE)

NOBILITY OF THOUGHT

29

Each day acquire something that will fortify you against poverty, against death, indeed against other misfortunes as well; and after you have run over many thoughts, select one to be thoroughly digested that day. This is my own custom; from the many things which I have read, I claim some one part for myself.

LUCIUS SENECA, *LETTERS FROM A STOIC*,
"II. ON DISCURSIVENESS IN READING" (FROM C. 63-65 CE)

The first thing which philosophy undertakes to give is fellow-feeling with all men; in other words, sympathy and sociability. We part company with our promise if we are unlike other men. We must see to it that the means by which we wish to draw admiration be not absurd and odious. Our motto, as you know, is "Live according to Nature"; but it is quite contrary to nature to torture the body, to hate unlaboured elegance, to be dirty on purpose, to eat food that is not only plain, but disgusting and forbidding. Just as it is a sign of luxury to seek out dainties, so it is madness to avoid that which is customary and can be purchased at no great price. Philosophy calls for plain living, but not for penance; and we may perfectly well be plain and neat at the same time. This is the mean of which I approve; our life should observe a happy medium between the ways of a sage and the ways of the world at large; all men should admire it, but they should understand it also.

LUCIUS SENECA, *LETTERS FROM A STOIC*, "V. ON THE PHILOSOPHER'S MEAN" (FROM C. 63-65 CE)

WISDOM

31

What a man applies himself to earnestly, that he naturally loves.
Do men then apply themselves earnestly to the things which
are bad? By no means. Well, do they apply themselves to things
which in no way concern themselves? Not to these either. It
remains then that they employ themselves earnestly only about
things which are good; and if they are earnestly employed about
things, they love such things also. Whoever then understands
what is good can also know how to love; but he who cannot
distinguish good from bad, and things which are neither good
nor bad from both, how can he possess the power of loving?
To love, then, is only in the power of the wise.

EPICTETUS, *THE TEACHINGS OF A STOIC:
SELECTED DISCOURSES AND THE ENCHIRIDION,*
"ON FRIENDSHIP" (FROM C. EARLY 2ND CENTURY CE)

VIRTUE

32

And if you ever wish to exercise yourself in labor and
endurance, do it for yourself, and not for others.

EPICTETUS, *THE TEACHINGS OF A STOIC: SELECTED
DISCOURSES AND THE ENCHIRIDION,* "THE MANUAL: XLVII"
(FROM C. EARLY 2ND CENTURY CE)

WILL

Where is the good? In the will. Where is the evil? In the will. Where is neither of them? In those things which are independent of the will.

EPICTETUS, *THE TEACHINGS OF A STOIC: SELECTED DISCOURSES AND THE ENCHIRIDION*, "THAT WE DO NOT STRIVE TO USE OUR OPINIONS ABOUT GOOD AND EVIL" (FROM C. EARLY 2ND CENTURY CE)

ACCEPTANCE

But not one of us chooses, even when necessity summons, readily to obey it, but weeping and groaning we suffer what we do suffer, and we call them "circumstances". What kind of circumstances, man? If you give the name of circumstances to the things which are around you, all things are circumstances; but if you call hardships by this name, what hardship is there in the dying of that which has been produced? But that which destroys is either a sword, or a wheel, or the sea, or a tile, or a tyrant. Why do you care about the way of going down to Hades? All ways are equal.

EPICTETUS, *THE TEACHINGS OF A STOIC: SELECTED DISCOURSES AND THE ENCHIRIDION*, "OF INDIFFERENCE" (FROM C. EARLY 2ND CENTURY CE)

DETACHMENT

...a man only loses that which he has. I have lost my garment. The reason is that you had a garment. I have a pain in my head. Have you any pain in your horns? Why then are you troubled? For we only lose those things, we have only pains about those things, which we possess.

EPICTETUS, *THE TEACHINGS OF A STOIC:*
SELECTED DISCOURSES AND THE ENCHIRIDION,
"THAT WE OUGHT NOT TO BE ANGRY WITH THE ERRORS
(FAULTS) OF OTHERS" (FROM C. EARLY 2ND CENTURY CE)

TIME

Though thou shouldst be going to live three thousand years, and as many times ten thousand years, still remember that no man loses any other life than this which he now lives, nor lives any other than this which he now loses. The longest and shortest are thus brought to the same. For the present is the same to all, though that which perishes is not the same; and so that which is lost appears to be a mere moment. For a man cannot lose either the past or the future: for what a man has not, how can anyone take this from him?

MARCUS AURELIUS, *MEDITATIONS*, "BOOK II" (FROM C. 180 CE)

TIME

37

Beasts avoid the dangers which they see, and when they have escaped them are free from care; but we men torment ourselves over that which is to come as well as over that which is past. Many of our blessings bring bane to us; for memory recalls the tortures of fear, while foresight anticipates them. The present alone can make no man wretched.

LUCIUS SENECA, *LETTERS FROM A STOIC*, "V. ON THE PHILOSOPHER'S MEAN" (FROM C. 63-65 CE)

WILL

38

What then should a man have in readiness in such circumstances? What else than this? What is mine, and what is not mine; and what is permitted to me, and what is not permitted to me. I must die. Must I then die lamenting? I must be put in chains. Must I then also lament? I must go into exile. Does any man then hinder me from going with smiles and cheerfulness and contentment?

EPICTETUS, *THE TEACHINGS OF A STOIC: SELECTED DISCOURSES AND THE ENCHIRIDION*, "OF THE THINGS WHICH ARE IN OUR POWER AND NOT IN OUR POWER" (FROM C. EARLY 2ND CENTURY CE)

VIRTUE

39

Labour not unwillingly, nor without regard to the common interest, nor without due consideration, nor with distraction; nor let studied ornament set off thy thoughts, and be not either a man of many words, or busy about too many things… Be cheerful also, and seek not external help nor the tranquility which others give. A man then must stand erect, not be kept erect by others.

MARCUS AURELIUS, *MEDITATIONS*, "BOOK III"
(FROM C. 180 CE)

WISDOM

40

There is a class of men who communicate, to anyone whom they meet, matters which should be revealed to friends alone, and unload upon the chance listener whatever irks them. Others, again, fear to confide in their closest intimates; and if it were possible, they would not trust even themselves, burying their secrets deep in their hearts. But we should do neither. It is equally faulty to trust everyone and to trust no one.

LUCIUS SENECA, *LETTERS FROM A STOIC*, "III.
ON TRUE AND FALSE FRIENDSHIP" (FROM C. 63-65 CE)

CHANGE

41

Thou art a little soul bearing about a corpse, as Epictetus used to say. It is no evil for things to undergo change, and no good for things to subsist in consequence of change. Time is like a river made up of the events which happen, and a violent stream; for as soon as a thing has been seen, it is carried away, and another comes in its place, and this will be carried away too. Everything which happens is as familiar and well known as the rose in spring and the fruit in summer; for such is disease, and death, and calumny, and treachery, and whatever else delights fools or vexes them. In the series of things those which follow are always aptly fitted to those which have gone before; for this series is not like a mere enumeration of disjointed things, which has only a necessary sequence, but it is a rational connection: and as all existing things are arranged together harmoniously, so the things which come into existence exhibit no mere succession, but a certain wonderful relationship.

MARCUS AURELIUS, *MEDITATIONS*, "BOOK IV" (FROM C. 180 CE)

DETACHMENT

We marvel at certain animals because they can pass through fire and suffer no bodily harm; but how much more marvellous is a man who has marched forth unhurt and unscathed through fire and sword and devastation! Do you understand now how much easier it is to conquer a whole tribe than to conquer one man? This saying of Stilbo makes common ground with Stoicism; the Stoic also can carry his goods unimpaired through cities that have been burned to ashes; for he is self-sufficient. Such are the bounds which he sets to his own happiness.

LUCIUS SENECA, *LETTERS FROM A STOIC*, "IX. ON PHILOSOPHY AND FRIENDSHIP" (FROM C. 63-65 CE)

VIRTUE

No man is able to borrow or buy a sound mind; in fact, as it seems to me, even though sound minds were for sale, they would not find buyers. Depraved minds, however, are bought and sold every day.

LUCIUS SENECA, *LETTERS FROM A STOIC*, "XXVII. ON THE GOOD WHICH ABIDES" (FROM C. 63-65 CE)

WILL

44

What then is education? Education is the learning how to adapt the natural præcognitions to the particular things conformably to nature; and then to distinguish that of things some are in our power, but others are not. In our power are will and all acts which depend on the will; things not in our power are the body, the parts of the body, possessions, parents, brothers, children, country, and, generally, all with whom we live in society. In what then should we place the good? To what kind of things shall we adapt it? To the things which are in our power? Is not health then a good thing, and soundness of limb, and life, and are not children and parents and country?

EPICTETUS, *THE TEACHINGS OF A STOIC: SELECTED DISCOURSES AND THE ENCHIRIDION*, "ON PRECOGNITIONS" (FROM C. EARLY 2ND CENTURY CE)

VIRTUE

45

Do not be carried along inconsiderately by the appearance of things, but give help to all according to thy ability and their fitness…

MARCUS AURELIUS, *MEDITATIONS*, "BOOK V" (FROM C. 180 CE)

VIRTUE

46

It is circumstances (difficulties) which show what men are.
Therefore when a difficulty falls upon you, remember that
God, like a trainer of wrestlers, has matched you with a rough
young man. For what purpose? you may say. Why, that you
may become an Olympic conqueror; but it is not accomplished
without sweat. In my opinion no man has had a more
profitable difficulty than you have had, if you choose to make
use of it as an athlete would deal with a young antagonist.

EPICTETUS, *THE TEACHINGS OF A STOIC:
SELECTED DISCOURSES AND THE ENCHIRIDION,*
"HOW WE SHOULD STRUGGLE WITH CIRCUMSTANCES"
(FROM C. EARLY 2ND CENTURY CE)

WISDOM

47

Because the gods have given the vine, or wheat, we sacrifice
to them; but because they have produced in the human mind
that fruit by which they designed to show us the truth which
relates to happiness, shall we not thank God for this?

EPICTETUS, *THE TEACHINGS OF A STOIC: SELECTED
DISCOURSES AND THE ENCHIRIDION,* "OF PROGRESS OR
IMPROVEMENT" (FROM C. EARLY 2ND CENTURY CE)

VIRTUE

For it is not because my ambition was rooted out that it has abated, but because it was wearied or perhaps even put out of temper by the failure of its plans. And so with luxury, also, which sometimes seems to have departed, and then when we have made a profession of frugality, begins to fret us and, amid our economies, seeks the pleasures which we have merely left but not condemned. Indeed, the more stealthily it comes, the greater is its force. For all unconcealed vices are less serious; a disease also is farther on the road to being cured when it breaks forth from concealment and manifests its power. So with greed, ambition, and the other evils of the mind – you may be sure that they do most harm when they are hidden behind a pretence of soundness.

LUCIUS SENECA, *LETTERS FROM A STOIC*, "LVI. ON QUIET AND STUDY" (FROM C. 63-65 CE)

TIME

Everything is only for a day, both that which remembers and that which is remembered.

MARCUS AURELIUS, *MEDITATIONS*, "BOOK IV" (FROM C. 180 CE)

DETACHMENT

50

Now that which does not make a man worse, how can it make a man's life worse? But neither through ignorance, nor having the knowledge, but not the power to guard against or correct these things, is it possible that the nature of the universe has overlooked them; nor is it possible that it has made so great a mistake, either through want of power or want of skill, that good and evil should happen indiscriminately to the good and the bad. But death certainly, and life, honour and dishonour, pain and pleasure, all these things equally happen to good men and bad, being things which make us neither better nor worse. Therefore they are neither good nor evil.

MARCUS AURELIUS, *MEDITATIONS*, "BOOK II" (FROM C. 180 CE)

VIRTUE

51

…nothing delights so much as the examples of the virtues, when they are exhibited in the morals of those who live with us and present themselves in abundance, as far as is possible. Wherefore we must keep them before us.

MARCUS AURELIUS, *MEDITATIONS*, "BOOK VI" (FROM C. 180 CE)

GOODNESS

52

All that is from the gods is full of Providence. That which is from fortune is not separated from nature or without an interweaving and involution with the things which are ordered by Providence. From thence all things flow; and there is besides necessity, and that which is for the advantage of the whole universe, of which thou art a part. But that is good for every part of nature which the nature of the whole brings, and what serves to maintain this nature. Now the universe is preserved, as by the changes of the elements so by the changes of things compounded of the elements. Let these principles be enough for thee, let them always be fixed opinions.

MARCUS AURELIUS, *MEDITATIONS*, "BOOK II" (FROM C. 180 CE)

ACCEPTANCE

53

Let death and exile and every other thing which appears dreadful be daily before your eyes; but most of all death: and you will never think of anything mean nor will you desire anything extravagantly.

EPICTETUS, *THE TEACHINGS OF A STOIC: SELECTED DISCOURSES AND THE ENCHIRIDION*, "THE MANUAL: XXI" (FROM C. EARLY 2ND CENTURY CE)

NOBILITY OF THOUGHT

You must linger among a limited number of master thinkers, and digest their works, if you would derive ideas which shall win firm hold in your mind. Everywhere means nowhere. When a person spends all his time in foreign travel, he ends by having many acquaintances, but no friends. And the same thing must hold true of men who seek intimate acquaintance with no single author, but visit them all in a hasty and hurried manner.

LUCIUS SENECA, *LETTERS FROM A STOIC,* "II. ON DISCURSIVENESS IN READING" (FROM C. 63-65 CE)

NOBILITY OF THOUGHT

Each day acquire something that will fortify you against poverty, against death, indeed against other misfortunes as well; and after you have run over many thoughts, select one to be thoroughly digested that day. This is my own custom; from the many things which I have read, I claim some one part for myself.

LUCIUS SENECA, *LETTERS FROM A STOIC,* "II. ON DISCURSIVENESS IN READING" (FROM C. 63-65 CE)

If he is a stranger to the universe who does not know what is in it, no less is he a stranger who does not know what is going on in it. He is a runaway, who flies from social reason; he is blind, who shuts the eyes of the understanding; he is poor, who has need of another, and has not from himself all things which are useful for life. He is an abscess on the universe who withdraws and separates himself from the reason of our common nature through being displeased with the things which happen, for the same nature produces this, and has produced thee too: he is a piece rent asunder from the state, who tears his own soul from that of reasonable animals, which is one.

MARCUS AURELIUS, *MEDITATIONS*, "BOOK IV" (FROM C. 180 CE)

If thou findest in human life anything better than justice, truth, temperance, fortitude, and, in a word, anything better than thy own mind's self-satisfaction in the things which it enables thee to do according to right reason, and in the condition that is assigned to thee without thy own choice; if, I say, thou seest anything better than this, turn to it with all thy soul, and enjoy that which thou hast found to be the best. But if nothing appears to be better than the deity which is planted in thee, which has subjected to itself all thy appetites, and carefully examines all the impressions, and, as Socrates said, has detached itself from the persuasions of sense, and has submitted itself to the gods, and cares for mankind; if thou findest everything else smaller and of less value than this, give place to nothing else, for if thou dost once diverge and incline to it, thou wilt no longer without distraction be able to give the preference to that good thing which is thy proper possession and thy own; for it is not right that anything of any other kind, such as praise from the many, or power, or enjoyment of pleasure, should come into competition with that which is rationally and politically or practically good.

MARCUS AURELIUS, *MEDITATIONS*, "BOOK III" (FROM C. 180 CE)

TIME

We ought to consider not only that our life is daily wasting away and a smaller part of it is left, but another thing also must be taken into the account, that if a man should live longer, it is quite uncertain whether the understanding will still continue sufficient for the comprehension of things, and retain the power of contemplation which strives to acquire the knowledge of the divine and the human… We must make haste then, not only because we are daily nearer to death, but also because the conception of things and the understanding of them cease first.

MARCUS AURELIUS, *MEDITATIONS*, "BOOK III" (FROM C. 180 CE)

WILL

Disease is an impediment to the body, but not to the will, unless the will itself chooses. Lameness is an impediment to the leg, but not to the will. And add this reflection on the occasion of everything that happens; for you will find it an impediment to something else, but not to yourself.

EPICTETUS, *THE TEACHINGS OF A STOIC: SELECTED DISCOURSES AND THE ENCHIRIDION*, "THE MANUAL: IX" (FROM C. EARLY 2ND CENTURY CE)

It is therefore enough for [animals] to eat and to drink, and to copulate, and to do all the other things which they severally do. But for us, to whom he has given also the intellectual faculty, these things are not sufficient; for unless we act in a proper and orderly manner, and conformably to the nature and constitution of each thing, we shall never attain our true end. For where the constitutions of living beings are different, there also the acts and the ends are different. In those animals then whose constitution is adapted only to use, use alone is enough; but in an animal (man), which has also the power of understanding the use, unless there be the due exercise of the understanding, he will never attain his proper end.

EPICTETUS, *THE TEACHINGS OF A STOIC: SELECTED DISCOURSES AND THE ENCHIRIDION*, "OF PROVIDENCE" (FROM C. EARLY 2ND CENTURY CE)

VIRTUE

Why will no man confess his faults? Because he is still in their grasp; only he who is awake can recount his dream, and similarly a confession of sin is a proof of sound mind. Let us, therefore, rouse ourselves, that we may be able to correct our mistakes. Philosophy, however, is the only power that can stir us, the only power that can shake off our deep slumber. Devote yourself wholly to philosophy. You are worthy of her; she is worthy of you; greet one another with a loving embrace. Say farewell to all other interests with courage and frankness. Do not study philosophy merely during your spare time.

LUCIUS SENECA, *LETTERS FROM A STOIC*, "LIII.
ON THE FAULTS OF THE SPIRIT" (FROM C. 63-65 CE)

DETACHMENT

To have whatsoever he wishes is in no man's power;
it is in his power not to wish for what he has not,
but cheerfully to employ what comes to him.

LUCIUS SENECA, *LETTERS FROM A STOIC*, "CXXIII.
ON THE CONFLICT BETWEEN PLEASURE AND VIRTUE"
(FROM C. 63-65 CE)

CHANGE

63

Death is such as generation is, a mystery of nature; a composition out of the same elements, and a decomposition into the same; and altogether not a thing of which any man should be ashamed, for it is not contrary to the nature of a reasonable animal, and not contrary to the reason of our constitution. It is natural that these things should be done by such persons, it is a matter of necessity; and if a man will not have it so, he will not allow the fig-tree to have juice. But by all means bear this in mind, that within a very short time both thou and he will be dead; and soon not even your names will be left behind.

MARCUS AURELIUS, *MEDITATIONS*, "BOOK IV" (FROM C. 180 CE)

VIRTUE

64

How hast thou behaved hitherto to the gods, thy parents, brethren, children, teachers, to those who looked after thy infancy, to thy friends, kinsfolk, to thy slaves? Consider if thou hast hitherto behaved to all in such a way that this may be said of thee: Never has wronged a man in deed or word.

MARCUS AURELIUS, *MEDITATIONS*, "BOOK V" (FROM C. 180 CE)

ACCEPTANCE

Whoever then clearly remembers this, that to man the measure of every act is the appearance (the opinion), whether the thing appears good or bad. If good, he is free from blame; if bad, himself suffers the penalty, for it is impossible that he who is deceived can be one person, and he who suffers another person – whoever remembers this will not be angry with any man, will not be vexed at any man, will not revile or blame any man, nor hate, nor quarrel with any man.

EPICTETUS, *THE TEACHINGS OF A STOIC: SELECTED DISCOURSES AND THE ENCHIRIDION*, "THAT WE OUGHT NOT TO BE ANGRY WITH MEN" (FROM C. EARLY 2ND CENTURY CE)

WISDOM

In short, if we observe, we shall find that the animal man is pained by nothing so much as by that which is irrational; and, on the contrary, attracted to nothing so much as to that which is rational.

EPICTETUS, *THE TEACHINGS OF A STOIC: SELECTED DISCOURSES AND THE ENCHIRIDION*, "HOW A MAN ON EVERY OCCASION CAN MAINTAIN HIS PROPER CHARACTER" (FROM C. EARLY 2ND CENTURY CE)

ACCEPTANCE

…there remains that which is peculiar to the good man, to be pleased and content with what happens, and with the thread which is spun for him; and not to defile the divinity which is planted in his breast, nor disturb it by a crowd of images, but to preserve it tranquil, following it obediently as a god, neither saying anything contrary to the truth, nor doing anything contrary to justice. And if all men refuse to believe that he lives a simple, modest, and contented life, he is neither angry with any of them, nor does he deviate from the way which leads to the end of life, to which a man ought to come pure, tranquil, ready to depart, and without any compulsion perfectly reconciled to his lot.

MARCUS AURELIUS, *MEDITATIONS*, "BOOK III" (FROM C. 180 CE)

TIME

Be not dissatisfied then that thou must live only so many years and not more; for as thou art satisfied with the amount of substance which has been assigned to thee, so be content with the time.

MARCUS AURELIUS, *MEDITATIONS*, "BOOK VI" (FROM C. 180 CE)

WISDOM

69

Would you really know what philosophy offers to humanity? Philosophy offers counsel. Death calls away one man, and poverty chafes another; a third is worried either by his neighbour's wealth or by his own. So-and-so is afraid of bad luck; another desires to get away from his own good fortune. Some are ill-treated by men, others by the gods. Why, then, do you frame for me such games as these? It is no occasion for jest; you are retained as counsel for unhappy mankind. You have promised to help those in peril by sea, those in captivity, the sick and the needy, and those whose heads are under the poised axe.

LUCIUS SENECA, *LETTERS FROM A STOIC*, "XLVIII. ON QUIBBLING AS UNWORTHY OF THE PHILOSOPHER" (FROM C. 63-65 CE)

VIRTUE

70

When thou hast been compelled by circumstances to be disturbed in a manner, quickly return to thyself and do not continue out of tune longer than the compulsion lasts; for thou wilt have more mastery over the harmony by continually recurring to it.

MARCUS AURELIUS, *MEDITATIONS*, "BOOK VI" (FROM C. 180 CE)

Men seek retreats for themselves, houses in the country, seashores, and mountains; and thou too art wont to desire such things very much. But this is altogether a mark of the most common sort of men, for it is in thy power whenever thou shalt choose to retire into thyself. For nowhere either with more quiet or more freedom from trouble does a man retire than into his own soul, particularly when he has within him such thoughts that by looking into them he is immediately in perfect tranquility; and I affirm that tranquility is nothing else than the good ordering of the mind. Constantly then give to thyself this retreat, and renew thyself; and let thy principles be brief and fundamental, which, as soon as thou shalt recur to them, will be sufficient to cleanse the soul completely, and to send thee back free from all discontent with the things to which thou returnest.

MARCUS AURELIUS, *MEDITATIONS*, "BOOK IV" (FROM C. 180 CE)

GOODNESS

This man who has been mistaken and deceived about the most important things, and blinded, not in the faculty of vision which distinguishes white and black, but in the faculty which distinguishes good and bad, should we not destroy him? If you speak thus you will see how inhuman this is which you say, and that it is just as if you would say, Ought we not to destroy this blind and deaf man? But if the greatest harm is the privation of the greatest things, and the greatest thing in every man is the will or choice such as it ought to be, and a man is deprived of this will, why are you also angry with him? Man, you ought not to be affected contrary to nature by the bad things of another. Pity him rather; drop this readiness to be offended and to hate, and these words which the many utter: "These accursed and odious fellows." How have you been made so wise at once? Why then are we angry?

EPICTETUS, *THE TEACHINGS OF A STOIC: SELECTED DISCOURSES AND THE ENCHIRIDION,* "THAT WE OUGHT NOT TO BE ANGRY WITH THE ERRORS (FAULTS) OF OTHERS" (FROM C. EARLY 2ND CENTURY CE)

CHANGE

Whatever this is that I am, it is a little flesh and breath, and the ruling part. Throw away thy books; no longer distract thyself: it is not allowed; but as if thou wast now dying, despise the flesh; it is blood and bones and a network, a contexture of nerves, veins, and arteries. See the breath also, what kind of a thing it is, air, and not always the same, but every moment sent out and again sucked in. The third then is the ruling part: consider thus: Thou art an old man; no longer let this be a slave, no longer be pulled by the strings like a puppet to unsocial movements, no longer either be dissatisfied with thy present lot, or shrink from the future.

MARCUS AURELIUS, *MEDITATIONS*, "BOOK II" (FROM C. 180 CE)

COOPERATION WITH NATURE

Does another do me wrong? Let him look to it. He has his own disposition, his own activity. I now have what the universal nature wills me to have; and I do what my nature now wills me to do.

MARCUS AURELIUS, *MEDITATIONS*, "BOOK V" (FROM C. 180 CE)

VIRTUE

75

…just as an engraver rests his eyes when they have long been under a strain and are weary, and calls them from their work, and "feasts" them, as the saying is; so we at times should slacken our minds and refresh them with some sort of entertainment. But let even your entertainment be work; and even from these various forms of entertainment you will select, if you have been watchful, something that may prove wholesome. That is my habit, Lucilius: I try to extract and render useful some element from every field of thought, no matter how far removed it may be from philosophy.

LUCIUS SENECA, *LETTERS FROM A STOIC*, "LVIII.
ON BEING" (FROM C. 63-65 CE)

VIRTUE

76

To consort with the crowd is harmful; there is no person who does not make some vice attractive to us, or stamp it upon us, or taint us unconsciously therewith. Certainly, the greater the mob with which we mingle, the greater the danger.

LUCIUS SENECA, *LETTERS FROM A STOIC*, "VII. ON
CROWDS" (FROM C. 63-65 CE)

NOBILITY OF THOUGHT

Respect means love, and love and fear cannot be mingled.

LUCIUS SENECA, *LETTERS FROM A STOIC*, "XLVII. ON MASTER AND SLAVE" (FROM C. 63-65 CE)

VIRTUE

Will you not perceive either what you are, or what you were born for, or what this is for which you have received the faculty of sight? But you may say, There are some things disagreeable and troublesome in life… have you not received faculties by which you will be able to bear all that happens? Have you not received greatness of soul? Have you not received manliness? Have you not received endurance? And why do I trouble myself about anything that can happen if I possess greatness of soul? What shall distract my mind, or disturb me, or appear painful? Shall I not use the power for the purposes for which I received it, and shall I grieve and lament over what happens?

EPICTETUS, *THE TEACHINGS OF A STOIC: SELECTED DISCOURSES AND THE ENCHIRIDION*, "OF PROVIDENCE" (FROM C. EARLY 2ND CENTURY CE)

GOODNESS

79

You cannot conceive what distinct progress I notice that each day brings to me. And when you say: "Give me also a share in these gifts which you have found so helpful," I reply that I am anxious to heap all these privileges upon you, and that I am glad to learn in order that I may teach. Nothing will ever please me, no matter how excellent or beneficial, if I must retain the knowledge of it to myself. And if wisdom were given me under the express condition that it must be kept hidden and not uttered, I should refuse it. No good thing is pleasant to possess, without friends to share it.

LUCIUS SENECA, *LETTERS FROM A STOIC,* "VI.
ON SHARING KNOWLEDGE" (FROM C. 63-65 CE)

VIRTUE

80

But he who values rational soul, a soul universal and fitted for political life, regards nothing else except this; and above all things he keeps his soul in a condition and in an activity conformable to reason and social life, and he cooperates to this end with those who are of the same kind as himself.

MARCUS AURELIUS, *MEDITATIONS,* "BOOK VI" (FROM C. 180 CE)

CHANGE

81

Remember to retire into this little territory of thy own, and above all do not distract or strain thyself, but be free, and look at things as a man, as a human being, as a citizen, as a mortal. But among the things readiest to thy hand to which thou shalt turn, let there be these, which are two. One is that things do not touch the soul, for they are external and remain immovable; but our perturbations come only from the opinion which is within. The other is that all these things, which thou seest, change immediately and will no longer be; and constantly bear in mind how many of these changes thou hast already witnessed. The universe is transformation: life is opinion.

MARCUS AURELIUS, *MEDITATIONS*, "BOOK IV" (FROM C. 180 CE)

TIME

82

What kind of people are those whom men wish to please, and for what objects, and by what kind of acts? How soon will time cover all things, and how many it has covered already.

MARCUS AURELIUS, *MEDITATIONS*, "BOOK VI" (FROM C. 180 CE)

…remember that you are a son. What does this character promise? To consider that everything which is the son's belongs to the father, to obey him in all things, never to blame him to another, nor to say or do anything which does him injury, to yield to him in all things and give way, co-operating with him as far as you can. After this know that you are a brother also, and that to this character it is due to make concessions; to be easily persuaded, to speak good of your brother, never to claim in opposition to him any of the things which are independent of the will, but readily to give them up, that you may have the larger share in what is dependent on the will. For see what a thing it is, in place of a lettuce, if it should so happen, or a seat, to gain for yourself goodness of disposition. How great is the advantage.

EPICTETUS, *THE TEACHINGS OF A STOIC:*
SELECTED DISCOURSES AND THE ENCHIRIDION,
"HOW WE MAY DISCOVER THE DUTIES OF LIFE FROM
NAMES" (FROM C. EARLY 2ND CENTURY CE)

NOBILITY OF THOUGHT

We ought then to check in the series of our thoughts everything that is without a purpose and useless, but most of all the overcurious feeling and the malignant...

MARCUS AURELIUS, *MEDITATIONS*, "BOOK III" (FROM C. 180 CE)

WISDOM

Cruelty usually follows wine-bibbing; for a man's soundness of mind is corrupted and made savage. Just as a lingering illness makes men querulous and irritable and drives them wild at the least crossing of their desires, so continued bouts of drunkenness bestialize the soul. For when people are often beside themselves, the habit of madness lasts on, and the vices which liquor generated retain their power even when the liquor is gone. Therefore you should state why the wise man ought not to get drunk. Explain by facts, and not by mere words, the hideousness of the thing, and its haunting evils. Do that which is easiest of all – namely, demonstrate that what men call pleasures are punishments as soon as they have exceeded due bounds.

LUCIUS SENECA, *LETTERS FROM A STOIC*, "LXXIX. ON DRUNKENNESS" (FROM C. 63-65 CE)

TIME

86

For with what art thou discontented? With the badness of men? Recall to thy mind this conclusion, that rational animals exist for one another, and that to endure is a part of justice, and that men do wrong involuntarily; and consider how many already, after mutual enmity, suspicion, hatred, and fighting, have been stretched dead, reduced to ashes; and be quiet at last…

MARCUS AURELIUS, *MEDITATIONS*, "BOOK IV" (FROM C. 180 CE)

ACCEPTANCE

87

Tell me where I can escape death; discover for me the country, show me the men to whom I must go, whom death does not visit. Discover to me a charm against death. If I have not one, what do you wish me to do? I cannot escape from death. Shall I not escape from the fear of death, but shall I die lamenting and trembling? For the origin of perturbation is this, to wish for something, and that this should not happen.

EPICTETUS, *THE TEACHINGS OF A STOIC:*
SELECTED DISCOURSES AND THE ENCHIRIDION,
"HOW WE SHOULD STRUGGLE WITH CIRCUMSTANCES"
(FROM C. EARLY 2ND CENTURY CE)

ACCEPTANCE

88

But now because we do not know the future, it is our duty to stick to the things which are in their nature more suitable for our choice, for we were made, among other things, for this.

EPICTETUS, *THE TEACHINGS OF A STOIC:*
SELECTED DISCOURSES AND THE ENCHIRIDION,
"HOW WE MAY DISCOVER THE DUTIES OF LIFE FROM
NAMES" (FROM C. EARLY 2ND CENTURY CE)

DETACHMENT

89

Go and salute a certain person. How? Not meanly. But I have been shut out, for I have not learned to make my way through the window; and when I have found the door shut, I must either come back or enter through the window. But still speak to him. In what way? Not meanly. But suppose that you have not got what you wanted. Was this your business, and not his? Why then do you claim that which belongs to another? Always remember what is your own, and what belongs to another; and you will not be disturbed.

EPICTETUS, *THE TEACHINGS OF A STOIC: SELECTED*
DISCOURSES AND THE ENCHIRIDION, "OF INDIFFERENCE"
(FROM C. EARLY 2ND CENTURY CE)

...to be instructed is this, to learn to wish that everything may happen as it does. And how do things happen? As the disposer has disposed them? And he has appointed summer and winter, and abundance and scarcity, and virtue and vice, and all such opposites for the harmony of the whole; and to each of us he has given a body, and parts of the body, and possessions, and companions... But you are unwilling to endure, and are discontented; and if you are alone, you call it solitude; and if you are with men, you call them knaves and robbers; and you find fault with your own parents and children, and brothers and neighbours. But you ought when you are alone to call this condition by the name of tranquillity and freedom, and to think yourself like to the gods; and when you are with many, you ought not to call it crowd, nor trouble, nor uneasiness, but festival and assembly, and so accept all contentedly.

EPICTETUS, *THE TEACHINGS OF A STOIC:*
SELECTED DISCOURSES AND THE ENCHIRIDION, "OF
CONTENTMENT" (FROM C. EARLY 2ND CENTURY CE)

WISDOM

91

"The wise man is self-sufficient." This phrase, my dear Lucilius, is incorrectly explained by many; for they withdraw the wise man from the world, and force him to dwell within his own skin. But we must mark with care what this sentence signifies and how far it applies; the wise man is sufficient unto himself for a happy existence, but not for mere existence. For he needs many helps towards mere existence; but for a happy existence he needs only a sound and upright soul, one that despises Fortune.

LUCIUS SENECA, *LETTERS FROM A STOIC*, "IX.
ON PHILOSOPHY AND FRIENDSHIP" (FROM C. 63-65 CE)

VIRTUE

92

One or two individuals will perhaps come in your way, but even these will have to be moulded and trained by you so that they will understand you. You may say: "For what purpose did I learn all these things?" But you need not fear that you have wasted your efforts; it was for yourself that you learned them.

LUCIUS SENECA, *LETTERS FROM A STOIC*, "VII.
ON CROWDS" (FROM C. 63-65 CE)

WISDOM

93

Any truth, I maintain, is my own property. And I shall continue to heap quotations from Epicurus upon you, so that all persons who swear by the words of another, and put a value upon the speaker and not upon the thing spoken, may understand that the best ideas are common property.

LUCIUS SENECA, *LETTERS FROM A STOIC*, "XII. ON OLD AGE" (FROM C. 63-65 CE)

GOODNESS

94

Plato, Aristotle, and the whole throng of sages who were destined to go each his different way, derived more benefit from the character than from the words of Socrates. It was not the classroom of Epicurus, but living together under the same roof, that made great men of Metrodorus, Hermarchus, and Polyaenus. Therefore I summon you, not merely that you may derive benefit, but that you may confer benefit; for we can assist each other greatly.

LUCIUS SENECA, *LETTERS FROM A STOIC*, "VI. ON SHARING KNOWLEDGE" (FROM C. 63-65 CE)

95

...everything which belongs to the body is a stream, and what belongs to the soul is a dream and vapour, and life is a warfare and a stranger's sojourn, and after-fame is oblivion. What then is that which is able to conduct a man? One thing and only one, philosophy. But this consists in keeping the daemon within a man free from violence and unharmed, superior to pains and pleasures, doing nothing without purpose, nor yet falsely and with hypocrisy, not feeling the need of another man's doing or not doing anything; and besides, accepting all that happens, and all that is allotted, as coming from thence, wherever it is, from whence he himself came; and, finally, waiting for death with a cheerful mind, as being nothing else than a dissolution of the elements of which every living being is compounded. But if there is no harm to the elements themselves in each continually changing into another, why should a man have any apprehension about the change and dissolution of all the elements? For it is according to nature, and nothing is evil which is according to nature.

MARCUS AURELIUS, *MEDITATIONS*, "BOOK II" (FROM C. 180 CE)

ACCEPTANCE

And here we conceive the work of a philosopher to be something of this kind: he must adapt his wish to what is going on, so that neither any of the things which are taking place shall take place contrary to our wish, nor any of the things which do not take place shall not take place when we wish that they should. From this the result is to those who have so arranged the work of philosophy, not to fail in the desire, nor to fall in with that which they would avoid; without uneasiness, without fear, without perturbation to pass through life themselves, together with their associates maintaining the relations both natural and acquired, as the relation of son, of father, of brother, of citizen, of man, of wife, of neighbour, of fellow-traveller, of ruler, of ruled. The work of a philosopher we conceive to be something like this.

EPICTETUS, *THE TEACHINGS OF A STOIC: SELECTED DISCOURSES AND THE ENCHIRIDION*, "TO NASO" (FROM C. EARLY 2ND CENTURY CE)

97

Never value anything as profitable to thyself which shall compel thee to break thy promise, to lose thy self respect, to hate any man, to suspect, to curse, to act the hypocrite, to desire anything which needs walls and curtains: for he who has preferred to everything intelligence and daemon and the worship of its excellence, acts no tragic part, does not groan, will not need either solitude or much company; and, what is chief of all, he will live without either pursuing or flying from death; but whether for a longer or a shorter time he shall have the soul enclosed in the body, he cares not at all: for even if he must depart immediately, he will go as readily as if he were going to do anything else which can be done with decency and order; taking care of this only all through life, that his thoughts turn not away from anything which belongs to an intelligent animal and a member of a civil community.

MARCUS AURELIUS, *MEDITATIONS*, "BOOK III"
(FROM C. 180 CE)

NOBILITY OF THOUGHT

98

But if you consider any man a friend whom you do not trust as you trust yourself, you are mightily mistaken and you do not sufficiently understand what true friendship means. Indeed, I would have you discuss everything with a friend; but first of all discuss the man himself. When friendship is settled, you must trust; before friendship is formed, you must pass judgment.

LUCIUS SENECA, *LETTERS FROM A STOIC*, "III. ON TRUE AND FALSE FRIENDSHIP" (FROM C. 63-65 CE)

CHANGE

99

I do not wish to involve myself in too large a question, and to discuss the treatment of slaves, towards whom we Romans are excessively haughty, cruel, and insulting. But this is the kernel of my advice: Treat your inferiors as you would be treated by your betters. And as often as you reflect how much power you have over a slave, remember that your master has just as much power over you. "But I have no master," you say. You are still young; perhaps you will have one.

LUCIUS SENECA, *LETTERS FROM A STOIC*, "XLVII. ON MASTER AND SLAVE" (FROM C. 63-65 CE)

DETACHMENT

Is any man then afraid about things which are not evils? No. Is he afraid about things which are evils, but still so far within his power that they may not happen? Certainly he is not. If then the things which are independent of the will are neither good nor bad, and all things which do depend on the will are within our power, and no man can either take them from us or give them to us, if we do not choose, where is room left for anxiety? But we are anxious about our poor body, our little property, about the will of Cæsar; but not anxious about things internal. Are we anxious about not forming a false opinion? No, for this is in my power. About not exerting our movements contrary to nature? No, not even about this.

EPICTETUS, *THE TEACHINGS OF A STOIC: SELECTED DISCOURSES AND THE ENCHIRIDION*, "ON ANXIETY (SOLICITUDE)" (FROM C. EARLY 2ND CENTURY CE)

VIRTUE

Since it is possible that thou mayest depart from life this very moment, regulate every act and thought accordingly.

MARCUS AURELIUS, *MEDITATIONS*, "BOOK II" (FROM C. 180 CE)

TIME

102

Our span of life is divided into parts; it consists of large circles enclosing smaller. One circle embraces and bounds the rest; it reaches from birth to the last day of existence. The next circle limits the period of our young manhood. The third confines all of childhood in its circumference. Again, there is, in a class by itself, the year; it contains within itself all the divisions of time by the multiplication of which we get the total of life. The month is bounded by a narrower ring. The smallest circle of all is the day; but even a day has its beginning and its ending, its sunrise and its sunset.

LUCIUS SENECA, *LETTERS FROM A STOIC*, "XII. ON OLD AGE" (FROM C. 63-65 CE)

ACCEPTANCE

103

Adapt thyself to the things with which thy lot has been cast: and the men among whom thou hast received thy portion, love them, but do it truly, sincerely.

MARCUS AURELIUS, *MEDITATIONS*, "BOOK VI" (FROM C. 180 CE)

VIRTUE

If thou workest at that which is before thee, following
right reason seriously, vigorously, calmly, without allowing
anything else to distract thee, but keeping thy divine
part pure, as if thou shouldst be bound to give it back
immediately; if thou holdest to this, expecting nothing,
fearing nothing, but satisfied with thy present activity
according to nature, and with heroic truth in every word
and sound which thou utterest, thou wilt live happy.
And there is no man who is able to prevent this.

MARCUS AURELIUS, *MEDITATIONS*, "BOOK III"
(FROM C. 180 CE)

GOODNESS

…you shall be told what pleased me today in the writings
of Hecato; it is these words: "What progress, you ask, have
I made? I have begun to be a friend to myself." That was
indeed a great benefit; such a person can never be alone.
You may be sure such a man is a friend to all mankind.

LUCIUS SENECA, *LETTERS FROM A STOIC*, "VI.
ON SHARING KNOWLEDGE" (FROM C. 63-65 CE)

DETACHMENT

And what is the divine law? To keep a man's own, not to claim that which belongs to others, but to use what is given, and when it is not given, not to desire it; and when a thing is taken away, to give it up readily and immediately, and to be thankful for the time that a man has had the use of it...

EPICTETUS, *THE TEACHINGS OF A STOIC: SELECTED DISCOURSES AND THE ENCHIRIDION*, "THAT WE DO NOT STRIVE TO USE OUR OPINIONS ABOUT GOOD AND EVIL" (FROM C. EARLY 2ND CENTURY CE)

TIME

...bear in mind that every man lives only this present time, which is an indivisible point, and that all the rest of his life is either past or it is uncertain. Short then is the time which every man lives, and small the nook of the earth where he lives; and short too the longest posthumous fame, and even this only continued by a succession of poor human beings, who will very soon die, and who know not even themselves, much less him who died long ago.

MARCUS AURELIUS, *MEDITATIONS*, "BOOK III" (FROM C. 180 CE)

TIME

… Heraclitus… remarked: "One day is equal to every day."
Different persons have interpreted the saying in different
ways. Some hold that days are equal in number of hours, and
this is true; for if by "day" we mean twenty-four hours' time,
all days must be equal, inasmuch as the night acquires what
the day loses. But others maintain that one day is equal to all
days through resemblance, because the very longest space of
time possesses no element which cannot be found in a single
day – namely, light and darkness – and even to eternity day
makes these alternations more numerous, not different when
it is shorter and different again when it is longer. Hence,
every day ought to be regulated as if it closed the series,
as if it rounded out and completed our existence.

LUCIUS SENECA, *LETTERS FROM A STOIC*, "XII. ON OLD AGE"
(FROM C. 63-65 CE)

VIRTUE

109

For universally, be not deceived, every animal is attached to nothing so much as to its own interests. Whatever then appears to it an impediment to this interest, whether this be a brother, or a father, or a child, or beloved, or lover, it hates, spurns, curses; for its nature is to love nothing so much as its own interests: this is father, and brother, and kinsman, and country, and God. When then the gods appear to us to be an impediment to this, we abuse them and throw down their statues and burn their temples, as Alexander ordered the temples of Aesculapius to be burned when his dear friend died. For this reason, if a man put in the same place his interest, sanctity, goodness, and country, and parents, and friends, all these are secured: but if he puts in one place his interest, in another his friends, and his country and his kinsmen and justice itself, all these give way, being borne down by the weight of interest.

EPICTETUS, *THE TEACHINGS OF A STOIC:
SELECTED DISCOURSES AND THE ENCHIRIDION,*
"ON FRIENDSHIP" (FROM C. EARLY 2ND CENTURY CE)

CHANGE

110

Let us cherish and love old age; for it is full of pleasure if one knows how to use it. Fruits are most welcome when almost over; youth is most charming at its close; the last drink delights the toper, the glass which souses him and puts the finishing touch on his drunkenness. Each pleasure reserves to the end the greatest delights which it contains. Life is most delightful when it is on the downward slope, but has not yet reached the abrupt decline. And I myself believe that the period which stands, so to speak, on the edge of the roof, possesses pleasures of its own. Or else the very fact of our not wanting pleasures has taken the place of the pleasures themselves. How comforting it is to have tired out one's appetites, and to have done with them!

LUCIUS SENECA, *LETTERS FROM A STOIC*, "XII.
ON OLD AGE" (FROM C. 63-65 CE)

TIME

111

Everything is only for a day, both that which remembers
and that which is remembered.

MARCUS AURELIUS, *MEDITATIONS*, "BOOK IV" (FROM C. 180 CE)

NOBILITY OF THOUGHT

A friend should be retained in the spirit; such a friend can never be absent. He can see every day whomsoever he desires to see. I would therefore have you share your studies with me, your meals, and your walks. We should be living within too narrow limits if anything were barred to our thoughts. I see you, my dear Lucilius, and at this very moment I hear you; I am with you to such an extent that I hesitate whether I should not begin to write you notes instead of letters.

LUCIUS SENECA, *LETTERS FROM A STOIC*, "LV. ON VATIA'S VILLA" (FROM C. 63-65 CE)

VIRTUE

...seeing that Providence rescues from its perils the world itself, which is no less mortal than we ourselves, that to some extent our petty bodies can be made to tarry longer upon earth by our own providence, if only we acquire the ability to control and check those pleasures whereby the greater portion of mankind perishes.

LUCIUS SENECA, *LETTERS FROM A STOIC*, "LVIII. ON BEING" (FROM C. 63-65 CE)

ACCEPTANCE

This is why the ancients taught the maxim, Know thyself. Therefore we ought to exercise ourselves in small things, and beginning with them to proceed to the greater. I have pain in the head. Do not say, Alas! I have pain in the ear. Do not say alas! And I do not say that you are not allowed to groan, but do not groan inwardly; and if your slave is slow in bringing a bandage, do not cry out and torment yourself, and say, Everybody hates me; for who would not hate such a man? For the future, relying on these opinions, walk about upright, free; not trusting to the size of your body, as an athlete, for a man ought not to be invincible in the way that an ass is.

EPICTETUS, *THE TEACHINGS OF A STOIC:*
SELECTED DISCOURSES AND THE ENCHIRIDION, "THAT WE
OUGHT NOT TO BE ANGRY WITH THE ERRORS (FAULTS)
OF OTHERS" (FROM C. EARLY 2ND CENTURY CE)

COOPERATION WITH NATURE

In conformity to the nature of the universe every single thing is accomplished…

MARCUS AURELIUS, *MEDITATIONS,* "BOOK VI" (FROM C. 180 CE)

…philosophy is a thing of holiness, something to be worshipped, so much so that the very counterfeit pleases. For the mass of mankind consider that a person is at leisure who has withdrawn from society, is free from care, self-sufficient, and lives for himself; but these privileges can be the reward only of the wise man. Does he who is a victim of anxiety know how to live for himself? What? Does he even know (and that is of first importance) how to live at all? For the man who has fled from affairs and from men, who has been banished to seclusion by the unhappiness which his own desires have brought upon him, who cannot see his neighbour more happy than himself, who through fear has taken to concealment, like a frightened and sluggish animal – this person is not living for himself, he is living for his belly, his sleep, and his lust – and that is the most shameful thing in the world. He who lives for no one does not necessarily live for himself.

LUCIUS SENECA, *LETTERS FROM A STOIC*,
"LV. ON VATIA'S VILLA" (FROM C. 63-65 CE)

GOODNESS

Observe then as thou hast begun; and whatever thou doest, do it in conjunction with this, the being good, and in the sense in which a man is properly understood to be good. Keep to this in every action. Do not have such an opinion of things as he has who does thee wrong, or such as he wishes thee to have, but look at them as they are in truth.

MARCUS AURELIUS, *MEDITATIONS*, "BOOK IV"
(FROM C. 180 CE)

WILL

We must therefore rouse ourselves to action and busy ourselves with interests that are good, as often as we are in the grasp of an uncontrollable sluggishness. Great generals, when they see that their men are mutinous, check them by some sort of labour or keep them busy with small forays. The much occupied man has no time for wantonness, and it is an obvious commonplace that the evils of leisure can be shaken off by hard work.

LUCIUS SENECA, *LETTERS FROM A STOIC*, "LVI
ON QUIET AND STUDY" (FROM C. 63-65 CE)

WISDOM

119

A man should always have these two rules in readiness; the one, to do only whatever the reason of the ruling and legislating faculty may suggest for the use of men; the other, to change thy opinion, if there is anyone at hand who sets thee right and moves thee from any opinion. But this change of opinion must proceed only from a certain persuasion, as of what is just or of common advantage, and the like, not because it appears pleasant or brings reputation. Hast thou reason? I have – why then dost not thou use it? For if this does its own work, what else dost thou wish? Thou hast existed as a part.

MARCUS AURELIUS, *MEDITATIONS*, "BOOK IV" (FROM C. 180 CE)

TIME

120

For what is a master? Man is not the master of man; but death is, and life and pleasure and pain; for if he comes without these things, bring Cæsar to me and you will see how firm I am.

EPICTETUS, *THE TEACHINGS OF A STOIC: SELECTED DISCOURSES AND THE ENCHIRIDION*, "ON CONSTANCY (OR FIRMNESS)" (FROM C. EARLY 2ND CENTURY CE)

I should like also to state to you one of the distinctions of Chrysippus, who declares that the wise man is in want of nothing, and yet needs many things. "On the other hand," he says, "nothing is needed by the fool, for he does not understand how to use anything, but he is in want of everything." The wise man needs hands, eyes, and many things that are necessary for his daily use; but he is in want of nothing. For want implies a necessity, and nothing is necessary to the wise man. Therefore, although he is self-sufficient, yet he has need of friends. He craves as many friends as possible, not, however, that he may live happily; for he will live happily even without friends. The Supreme Good calls for no practical aids from outside; it is developed at home, and arises entirely within itself. If the good seeks any portion of itself from without, it begins to be subject to the play of Fortune.

LUCIUS SENECA, *LETTERS FROM A STOIC*, "IX. ON PHILOSOPHY AND FRIENDSHIP" (FROM C. 63-65 CE)

WILL

The being (nature) of the good is a certain will; the being of the bad is a certain kind of will. What, then, are externals? Materials for the will, about which the will being conversant shall obtain its own good or evil. How shall it obtain the good? If it does not admire (over-value) the materials; for the opinions about the materials, if the opinions are right, make the will good: but perverse and distorted opinions make the will bad. God has fixed this law, and says, "If you would have anything good, receive it from yourself." You say, No, but I will have it from another. Do not so: but receive it from yourself.

EPICTETUS, *THE TEACHINGS OF A STOIC: SELECTED DISCOURSES AND THE ENCHIRIDION*, "ON CONSTANCY (OR FIRMNESS)" (FROM C. EARLY 2ND CENTURY CE)

DETACHMENT

I do my duty: other things trouble me not; for they are either things without life, or things without reason, or things that have rambled and know not the way.

MARCUS AURELIUS, *MEDITATIONS*, "BOOK VI" (FROM C. 180 CE)

DETACHMENT

In some such way as this the sage will act; he will retreat into himself, and live with himself. As long as he is allowed to order his affairs according to his judgment, he is self-sufficient – and marries a wife; he is self-sufficient – and brings up children; he is self-sufficient – and yet could not live if he had to live without the society of man. Natural promptings, and not his own selfish needs, draw him into Friendships.

LUCIUS SENECA, *LETTERS FROM A STOIC*, "IX. ON PHILOSOPHY AND FRIENDSHIP" (FROM C. 63-65 CE)

GOODNESS

God is near you, he is with you, he is within you. This is what I mean, Lucilius: a holy spirit indwells within us, one who marks our good and bad deeds, and is our guardian. As we treat this spirit, so are we treated by it. Indeed, no man can be good without the help of God. Can one rise superior to fortune unless God helps him to rise? He it is that gives noble and upright counsel.

LUCIUS SENECA, *LETTERS FROM A STOIC*, "XLI. ON THE GOD WITHIN US" (FROM C. 63-65 CE)

How quickly all things disappear, in the universe the bodies themselves, but in time the remembrance of them; what is the nature of all sensible things, and particularly those which attract with the bait of pleasure or terrify by pain, or are noised abroad by vapoury fame; how worthless, and contemptible, and sordid, and perishable, and dead they are – all this it is the part of the intellectual faculty to observe. To observe too who these are whose opinions and voices give reputation; what death is, and the fact that, if a man looks at it in itself, and by the abstractive power of reflection resolves into their parts all the things which present themselves to the imagination in it, he will then consider it to be nothing else than an operation of nature; and if anyone is afraid of an operation of nature, he is a child. This, however, is not only an operation of nature, but it is also a thing which conduces to the purposes of nature.

MARCUS AURELIUS, *MEDITATIONS*, "BOOK II" (FROM C. 180 CE)

CHANGE

…rejoice in that which is present and be content with the things which come in season. If you see anything which you have learned and inquired about occurring to you in your course of life (or opportunely applied by you to the acts of life), be delighted at it… if you are not moved by what you formerly were, and not in the same way as you once were, you can celebrate a festival daily – today because you have behaved well in one act, and tomorrow because you have behaved well in another.

EPICTETUS, *THE TEACHINGS OF A STOIC: SELECTED DISCOURSES AND THE ENCHIRIDION*, "TO THOSE WHO ARE DESIROUS OF PASSING LIFE IN TRANQUILITY" (FROM C. EARLY 2ND CENTURY CE)

GOODNESS

Look within. Within is the fountain of good, and it will ever bubble up, if thou wilt ever dig.

MARCUS AURELIUS, *MEDITATIONS*, "BOOK VII" (FROM C. 180 CE)

"A man may rule the world and still be unhappy, if he does not feel that he is supremely happy." In order, however, that you may know that these sentiments are universal, suggested, of course, by Nature, you will find in one of the comic poets this verse: "Unblest is he who thinks himself unblest," or what does your condition matter, if it is bad in your own eyes? You may say: "What then? If yonder man, rich by base means, and yonder man, lord of many but slave of more, shall call themselves happy, will their own opinion make them happy?" It matters not what one says, but what one feels; also, not how one feels on one particular day, but how one feels at all times. There is no reason, however, why you should fear that this great privilege will fall into unworthy hands; only the wise man is pleased with his own. Folly is ever troubled with weariness of itself.

LUCIUS SENECA, *LETTERS FROM A STOIC*, "IX.
ON PHILOSOPHY AND FRIENDSHIP" (FROM C. 63-65 CE)

But if you ask me what then is the most excellent of all things, what must I say? I cannot say the power of speaking, but the power of the will, when it is right. For it is this which uses the other (the power of speaking), and all the other faculties both small and great. For when this faculty of the will is set right, a man who is not good becomes good: but when it fails, a man becomes bad. It is through this that we are unfortunate, that we are fortunate, that we blame one another, are pleased with one another. In a word, it is this which if we neglect it makes unhappiness, and if we carefully look after it, makes happiness.

EPICTETUS, *THE TEACHINGS OF A STOIC: SELECTED DISCOURSES AND THE ENCHIRIDION*, "ON THE POWER OF SPEAKING" (FROM C. EARLY 2ND CENTURY CE)

TIME

These two things then thou must bear in mind; the one, that all things from eternity are of like forms and come round in a circle, and that it makes no difference whether a man shall see the same things during a hundred years or two hundred, or an infinite time; and the second, that the longest liver and he who will die soonest lose just the same. For the present is the only thing of which a man can be deprived, if it is true that this is the only thing which he has, and that a man cannot lose a thing if he has it not.

MARCUS AURELIUS, *MEDITATIONS*, "BOOK II" (FROM C. 180 CE)

NOBILITY OF THOUGHT

Learn my opinions: show me yours; and then say that you have visited me. Let us examine one another: if I have any bad opinion, take it away; if you have any, show it. This is the meaning of meeting with a philosopher.

EPICTETUS, *THE TEACHINGS OF A STOIC: SELECTED DISCOURSES AND THE ENCHIRIDION*, "TO A CERTAIN RHETORICIAN WHO WAS GOING UP TO ROME ON A SUIT" (FROM C. EARLY 2ND CENTURY CE)

CHANGE

Frugal living can bring one to old age; and to my mind old age is not to be refused any more than is to be craved. There is a pleasure in being in one's own company as long as possible, when a man has made himself worth enjoying. The question, therefore, on which we have to record our judgment is, whether one should shrink from extreme old age and should hasten the end artificially, instead of waiting for it to come. A man who sluggishly awaits his fate is almost a coward, just as he is immoderately given to wine who drains the jar dry and sucks up even the dregs. But we shall ask this question also: "Is the extremity of life the dregs, or is it the clearest and purest part of all, provided only that the mind is unimpaired, and the senses, still sound, give their support to the spirit, and the body is not worn out and dead before its time?"

LUCIUS SENECA, *LETTERS FROM A STOIC*, "LVIII. ON BEING" (FROM C. 63-65 CE)

COOPERATION WITH NATURE

134

The soul of man does violence to itself, first of all, when it becomes an abscess and, as it were, a tumour on the universe, so far as it can. For to be vexed at anything which happens is a separation of ourselves from nature, in some part of which the natures of all other things are contained. In the next place, the soul does violence to itself when it turns away from any man, or even moves towards him with the intention of injuring, such as are the souls of those who are angry. In the third place, the soul does violence to itself when it is overpowered by pleasure or by pain. Fourthly, when it plays a part, and does or says anything insincerely and untruly. Fifthly, when it allows any act of its own and any movement to be without an aim, and does anything thoughtlessly and without considering what it is, it being right that even the smallest things be done with reference to an end; and the end of rational animals is to follow the reason...

MARCUS AURELIUS, *MEDITATIONS*, "BOOK II"
(FROM C. 180 CE)

WILL

135

For if you wish to maintain a will conformable to nature, you have every security, every facility, you have no troubles. For if you wish to maintain what is in your own power and is naturally free, and if you are content with these, what else do you care for? For who is the master of such things? Who can take them away? If you choose to be modest and faithful, who shall not allow you to be so? If you choose not to be restrained or compelled, who shall compel you to desire what you think that you ought not to desire? Who shall compel you to avoid what you do not think fit to avoid?

EPICTETUS, *THE TEACHINGS OF A STOIC: SELECTED DISCOURSES AND THE ENCHIRIDION*, "OF TRANQUILITY (FREEDOM FROM PERTURBATION)" (FROM C. EARLY 2ND CENTURY CE)

VIRTUE

136

Above, below, all around are the movements of the elements. But the motion of virtue is in none of these: it is something more divine, and advancing by a way hardly observed it goes happily on its road.

MARCUS AURELIUS, *MEDITATIONS*, "BOOK VI" (FROM C. 180 CE)

COOPERATION WITH NATURE

It is no common (easy) thing to do this only, to fulfil the promise of a man's nature. For what is a man? The answer is, A rational and mortal being. Then by the rational faculty from whom are we separated? From wild beasts. And from what others? From sheep and like animals. Take care then to do nothing like a wild beast; but if you do, you have lost the character of a man; you have not fulfilled your promise. See that you do nothing like a sheep; but if you do, in this case also the man is lost. What then do we do as sheep? When we act gluttonously, when we act lewdly, when we act rashly, filthily, inconsiderately, to what have we declined? To sheep.

What have we lost? The rational faculty. When we act contentiously and harmfully and passionately and violently, to what have we declined? To wild beasts.

EPICTETUS, *THE TEACHINGS OF A STOIC: SELECTED DISCOURSES AND THE ENCHIRIDION*, "THAT WHEN WE CANNOT FULFIL THAT WHICH THE CHARACTER OF A MAN PROMISES, WE ASSUME THE CHARACTER OF A PHILOSOPHER" (FROM C. EARLY 2ND CENTURY CE)

COOPERATION WITH NATURE

How, even if my brother is not reconciled to me, shall I maintain myself in a state conformable to nature? Nothing great, said Epictetus, is produced suddenly, since not even the grape or the fig is. If you say to me now that you want a fig, I will answer to you that it requires time: let it flower first, then put forth fruit, and then ripen. Is then the fruit of a fig-tree not perfected suddenly and in one hour, and would you possess the fruit of a man's mind in so short a time and so easily? Do not expect it, even if I tell you.

EPICTETUS, *THE TEACHINGS OF A STOIC: SELECTED DISCOURSES AND THE ENCHIRIDION*, "WHAT PHILOSOPHY PROMISES" (FROM C. EARLY 2ND CENTURY CE)

WILL

Things themselves touch not the soul, not in the least degree; nor have they admission to the soul, nor can they turn or move the soul: but the soul turns and moves itself alone, and whatever judgements it may think proper to make, such it makes for itself the things which present themselves to it.

MARCUS AURELIUS, *MEDITATIONS*, "BOOK V" (FROM C. 180 CE)

Show those qualities then which are altogether in thy power, sincerity, gravity, endurance of labour, aversion to pleasure, contentment with thy portion and with few things, benevolence, frankness, no love of superfluity, freedom from trifling magnanimity. Dost thou not see how many qualities thou art immediately able to exhibit, in which there is no excuse of natural incapacity and unfitness, and yet thou still remainest voluntarily below the mark? Or art thou compelled through being defectively furnished by nature to murmur, and to be stingy, and to flatter, and to find fault with thy poor body, and to try to please men, and to make great display, and to be so restless in thy mind? No, by the gods: but thou mightest have been delivered from these things long ago. Only if in truth thou canst be charged with being rather slow and dull of comprehension, thou must exert thyself about this also, not neglecting it nor yet taking pleasure in thy dullness.

MARCUS AURELIUS, *MEDITATIONS*, "BOOK V" (FROM C. 180 CE)

I can only say this to you, that he who knows not who he is, and for what purpose he exists, and what is this world, and with whom he is associated, and what things are the good and the bad, and the beautiful and the ugly, and who neither understands discourse nor demonstration, nor what is true nor what is false, and who is not able to distinguish them, will neither desire according to nature nor turn away nor move towards, nor intend (to act), nor assent, nor dissent, nor suspend his judgment: to say all in a few words, he will go about dumb and blind, thinking that he is somebody, but being nobody. Is this so now for the first time? Is it not the fact that ever since the human race existed, all errors and misfortunes have arisen through this ignorance?

EPICTETUS, *THE TEACHINGS OF A STOIC: SELECTED DISCOURSES AND THE ENCHIRIDION*, "TO (OR AGAINST) A PERSON WHO WAS ONE OF THOSE WHO WERE NOT VALUED (ESTEEMED) BY HIM" (FROM C. EARLY 2ND CENTURY CE)

CHANGE

142

Socrates made the same remark to one who complained; he said: "Why do you wonder that globe-trotting does not help you, seeing that you always take yourself with you? The reason which set you wandering is ever at your heels." What pleasure is there in seeing new lands? Or in surveying cities and spots of interest? All your bustle is useless. Do you ask why such flight does not help you? It is because you flee along with yourself. You must lay aside the burdens of the mind; until you do this, no place will satisfy you.

LUCIUS SENECA, *LETTERS FROM A STOIC*, "XXVIII. ON TRAVEL AS A CURE FOR DISCONTENT" (FROM C. 63-65 CE)

NOBILITY OF THOUGHT

143

Such as are thy habitual thoughts, such also will be the character of thy mind; for the soul is dyed by the thoughts. Dye it then with a continuous series of such thoughts as these: for instance, that where a man can live, there he can also live well.

MARCUS AURELIUS, *MEDITATIONS*, "BOOK V" (FROM C. 180 CE)

ACCEPTANCE

144

For two reasons then it is right to be content with that which happens to thee; the one, because it was done for thee and prescribed for thee, and in a manner had reference to thee, originally from the most ancient causes spun with thy destiny; and the other, because even that which comes severally to every man is to the power which administers the universe a cause of felicity and perfection, nay even of its very continuance. For the integrity of the whole is mutilated, if thou cuttest off anything whatever from the conjunction and the continuity either of the parts or of the causes. And thou dost cut off, as far as it is in thy power, when thou art dissatisfied, and in a manner triest to put anything out of the way.

MARCUS AURELIUS, *MEDITATIONS*, "BOOK V" (FROM C. 180 CE)

WISDOM

145

...if any man is able to convince me and show me that I do not think or act right, I will gladly change; for I seek the truth by which no man was ever injured. But he is injured who abides in his error and ignorance.

MARCUS AURELIUS, *MEDITATIONS*, "BOOK VI" (FROM C. 180 CE)

WISDOM

Observe whom you yourself praise, when you praise many persons without partiality: do you praise the just or the unjust? The just. Whether do you praise the moderate or the immoderate? The moderate. And the temperate or the intemperate? The temperate. If then you make yourself such a person, you will know that you will make yourself beautiful; but so long as you neglect these things, you must be ugly, even though you contrive all you can to appear beautiful.

EPICTETUS, *THE TEACHINGS OF A STOIC: SELECTED DISCOURSES AND THE ENCHIRIDION*, "OF FINERY IN DRESS" (FROM C. EARLY 2ND CENTURY CE)

CHANGE

…yield not to adversity; trust not to prosperity; keep before your eyes the full scope of Fortune's power, as if she would surely do whatever is in her power to do. That which has been long expected comes more gently.

LUCIUS SENECA, *LETTERS FROM A STOIC*, "LXXVIII. ON THE HEALING POWER OF THE MIND" (FROM C. 63-65 CE)

I feel that age has done no damage to my mind, though I feel its effects on my constitution. Only my vices, and the outward aids to these vices, have reached senility; my mind is strong and rejoices that it has but slight connection with the body. It has laid aside the greater part of its load. It is alert; it takes issue with me on the subject of old age; it declares that old age is its time of bloom. Let me take it at its word, and let it make the most of the advantages it possesses. The mind bids me do some thinking and consider how much of this peace of spirit and moderation of character I owe to wisdom and how much to my time of life; it bids me distinguish carefully what I cannot do and what I do not want to do. . . For why should one complain or regard it as a disadvantage, if powers which ought to come to an end have failed?

LUCIUS SENECA, *LETTERS FROM A STOIC*, "XXVII. ON OLD AGE AND DEATH" (FROM C. 63-65 CE)

Be not disgusted, nor discouraged, nor dissatisfied, if thou dost not succeed in doing everything according to right principles; but when thou hast failed, return back again, and be content if the greater part of what thou doest is consistent with man's nature, and love this to which thou returnest; and do not return to philosophy as if she were a master… For thus thou wilt not fail to obey reason, and thou wilt repose in it. And remember that philosophy requires only the things which thy nature requires; but thou wouldst have something else which is not according to nature – It may be objected, Why what is more agreeable than this which I am doing? – But is not this the very reason why pleasure deceives us? And consider if magnanimity, freedom, simplicity, equanimity, piety, are not more agreeable. For what is more agreeable than wisdom itself, when thou thinkest of the security and the happy course of all things which depend on the faculty of understanding and knowledge?

MARCUS AURELIUS, *MEDITATIONS*, "BOOK V" (FROM C. 180 CE)

NOBILITY OF THOUGHT

150

Since then it is of necessity that every man uses everything according to the opinion which he has about it, those, the few, who think that they are formed for fidelity and modesty and a sure use of appearances have no mean or ignoble thoughts about themselves; but with the many it is quite the contrary. For they say, What am I? A poor, miserable man, with my wretched bit of flesh. Wretched, indeed; but you possess something better than your bit of flesh. Why then do you neglect that which is better, and why do you attach yourself to this?

EPICTETUS, *THE TEACHINGS OF A STOIC: SELECTED DISCOURSES AND THE ENCHIRIDION*, "HOW A MAN SHOULD PROCEED FROM THE PRINCIPLE OF GOD BEING THE FATHER OF ALL MEN TO THE REST" (FROM C. EARLY 2ND CENTURY CE)

WISDOM

151

Examine men's ruling principles, even those of the wise, what kind of things they avoid, and what kind they pursue.

MARCUS AURELIUS, *MEDITATIONS*, "BOOK IV" (FROM C. 180 CE)

VIRTUE

152

"Ungoverned anger begets madness." You cannot help knowing the truth of these words, since you have had not only slaves, but also enemies. But indeed this emotion blazes out against all sorts of persons; it springs from love as much as from hate, and shows itself not less in serious matters than in jest and sport. And it makes no difference how important the provocation may be, but into what kind of soul it penetrates. Similarly with fire; it does not matter how great is the flame, but what it falls upon. For solid timbers have repelled a very great fire; conversely, dry and easily inflammable stuff nourishes the slightest spark into a conflagration. So it is with anger, my dear Lucilius; the outcome of a mighty anger is madness, and hence anger should be avoided, not merely that we may escape excess, but that we may have a healthy mind.

LUCIUS SENECA, *LETTERS FROM A STOIC*, "XVIII.
ON FESTIVALS AND FASTING" (FROM C. 63-65 CE)

DETACHMENT

It is peculiar to man to love even those who do wrong.
And this happens, if when they do wrong it occurs to thee
that they are kinsmen, and that they do wrong through
ignorance and unintentionally, and that soon both of you
will die; and above all, that the wrongdoer has done thee
no harm, for he has not made thy ruling faculty worse
than it was before.

MARCUS AURELIUS, *MEDITATIONS*, "BOOK VII" (FROM C. 180 CE)

GOODNESS

But indeed for the power of seeing and hearing, and
indeed for life itself, and for the things which contribute
to support it, for the fruits which are dry, and for wine
and oil give thanks to God: but remember that he has
given you something else better than all these, I mean
the power of using them, proving them, and
estimating the value of each.

EPICTETUS, *THE TEACHINGS OF A STOIC: SELECTED
DISCOURSES AND THE ENCHIRIDION*, "ON THE POWER OF
SPEAKING" (FROM C. EARLY 2ND CENTURY CE)

ACCEPTANCE

The thought for today is one which I discovered in Epicurus; for I am wont to cross over even into the enemy's camp – not as a deserter, but as a scout. He says: "Contented poverty is an honourable estate." Indeed, if it be contented, it is not poverty at all. It is not the man who has too little, but the man who craves more, that is poor.

LUCIUS SENECA, *LETTERS FROM A STOIC*, "II. ON DISCURSIVENESS IN READING" (FROM C. 63-65 CE)

WILL

For I force my mind to concentrate, and keep it from straying to things outside itself; all outdoors may be bedlam, provided that there is no disturbance within, provided that fear is not wrangling with desire in my breast, provided that meanness and lavishness are not at odds, one harassing the other. For of what benefit is a quiet neighbourhood, if our emotions are in an uproar?

LUCIUS SENECA, *LETTERS FROM A STOIC*, "LVI. ON QUIET AND STUDY" (FROM C. 63-65 CE)

COOPERATION WITH NATURE

…it is a man's duty to comfort himself, and to wait for the natural dissolution and not to be vexed at the delay, but to rest in these principles only: the one, that nothing will happen to me which is not conformable to the nature of the universe; and the other, that it is in my power never to act contrary to my god and daemon: for there is no man who will compel me to this.

MARCUS AURELIUS, *MEDITATIONS*, "BOOK V" (FROM C. 180 CE)

DETACHMENT

[Diogenes] says that death is no evil, for neither is it base; he says that fame (reputation) is the noise of madmen. And what… about pain, about pleasure, and about poverty? He says that to be naked is better than any purple robe, and to sleep on the bare ground is the softest bed; and he gives as a proof of each thing that he affirms his own courage, his tranquillity, his freedom, and the healthy appearance and compactness of his body.
There is no enemy near, he says; all is peace.

EPICTETUS, *THE TEACHINGS OF A STOIC: SELECTED DISCOURSES AND THE ENCHIRIDION*, "HOW WE SHOULD STRUGGLE WITH CIRCUMSTANCES" (FROM C. EARLY 2ND CENTURY CE)

For what is weeping and lamenting? Opinion. What is bad
fortune? Opinion. What is civil sedition, what is divided
opinion, what is blame, what is accusation, what is impiety,
what is trifling? All these things are opinions, and nothing
more, and opinions about things independent of the will, as
if they were good and bad. Let a man transfer these opinions
to things dependent on the will, and I engage for him that
he will be firm and constant, whatever may be the state of
things around him. Such as is a dish of water, such is the
soul. Such as is the ray of light which falls on the water, such
are the appearances. When the water is moved, the ray also
seems to be moved, yet it is not moved. And when then a
man is seized with giddiness, it is not the arts and the virtues
which are confounded, but the spirit (the nervous power) on
which they are impressed; but if the spirit be restored to
its settled state, those things also are restored.

EPICTETUS, *THE TEACHINGS OF A STOIC:
SELECTED DISCOURSES AND THE ENCHIRIDION*, "WHAT
IS THE MATTER ON WHICH A GOOD MAN SHOULD BE
EMPLOYED, AND IN WHAT WE OUGHT CHIEFLY TO PRACTISE
OURSELVES" (FROM C. EARLY 2ND CENTURY CE)

Those who have never attained their mental independence begin, in the first place, by following the leader in cases where everyone has deserted the leader; then, in the second place, they follow him in matters where the truth is still being investigated. However, the truth will never be discovered if we rest contented with discoveries already made. Besides, he who follows another not only discovers nothing but is not even investigating. What then? Shall I not follow in the footsteps of my predecessors? I shall indeed use the old road, but if I find one that makes a shorter cut and is smoother to travel, I shall open the new road. Men who have made these discoveries before us are not our masters, but our guides. Truth lies open for all; it has not yet been monopolized. And there is plenty of it left even for posterity to discover.

LUCIUS SENECA, *LETTERS FROM A STOIC*, "XXXIII. ON THE FUTILITY OF LEARNING MAXIMS" (FROM C. 63-65 CE)

WISDOM

The material for the wise and good man is his own ruling faculty: and the body is the material for the physician and the aliptes (the man who oils persons); the land is the matter for the husbandman. The business of the wise and good man is to use appearances conformably to nature: and as it is the nature of every soul to assent to the truth, to dissent from the false, and to remain in suspense as to that which is uncertain; so it is its nature to be moved towards the desire for the good, and to aversion from the evil; and with respect to that which is neither good nor bad it feels indifferent.

EPICTETUS, *THE TEACHINGS OF A STOIC: SELECTED DISCOURSES AND THE ENCHIRIDION*, "WHAT IS THE MATTER ON WHICH A GOOD MAN SHOULD BE EMPLOYED, AND IN WHAT WE OUGHT CHIEFLY TO PRACTISE OURSELVES" (FROM C. EARLY 2ND CENTURY CE)

CHANGE

Asia, Europe are corners of the universe: all the sea a drop in the universe; Athos a little clod of the universe: all the present time is a point in eternity. All things are little, changeable, perishable.

MARCUS AURELIUS, *MEDITATIONS*, "BOOK VI" (FROM C. 180 CE)

DETACHMENT

If you see a man who is unterrified in the midst of dangers, untouched by desires, happy in adversity, peaceful amid the storm, who looks down upon men from a higher plane, and views the gods on a footing of equality, will not a feeling of reverence for him steal over you, will you not say: "This quality is too great and too lofty to be regarded as resembling this petty body in which it dwells? A divine power has descended upon that man."

LUCIUS SENECA, *LETTERS FROM A STOIC*, "XLI. ON THE GOD WITHIN US" (FROM C. 63-65 CE)

NOBILITY OF THOUGHT

Know you not how small a part you are compared with the whole. I mean with respect to the body, for as to intelligence you are not inferior to the gods nor less; for the magnitude of intelligence is not measured by length nor yet by height, but by thoughts.

EPICTETUS, *THE TEACHINGS OF A STOIC: SELECTED DISCOURSES AND THE ENCHIRIDION*, "OF PROVIDENCE" (FROM C. EARLY 2ND CENTURY CE)

GOODNESS

When the good appears, it immediately attracts to itself;
the evil repels from itself. But the soul will never reject the
manifest appearance of the good, any more than persons
will reject Cæsar's coin. On this principle depends every
movement both of man and God.

EPICTETUS, *THE TEACHINGS OF A STOIC: SELECTED
DISCOURSES AND THE ENCHIRIDION*, "WHAT IS THE MATTER
ON WHICH A GOOD MAN SHOULD BE EMPLOYED, AND IN
WHAT WE OUGHT CHIEFLY TO PRACTISE OURSELVES"
(FROM C. EARLY 2ND CENTURY CE)

DETACHMENT

For he alone is in kinship with God who has scorned wealth.
Of course I do not forbid you to possess it, but I would have
you reach the point at which you possess it dauntlessly;
this can be accomplished only by persuading yourself that
you can live happily without it as well as with it, and by
regarding riches always as likely to elude you.

LUCIUS SENECA, *LETTERS FROM A STOIC*, "XVIII. ON
FESTIVALS AND FASTING" (FROM C. 63-65 CE)

GOODNESS

What kind of things those are which appear good to the many, we may learn even from this. For if any man should conceive certain things as being really good, such as prudence, temperance, justice, fortitude, he would not after having first conceived these endure to listen to anything which should not be in harmony with what is really good.

MARCUS AURELIUS, *MEDITATIONS*, "BOOK V" (FROM C. 180 CE)

CHANGE

Do you suppose that you alone have had this experience? Are you surprised, as if it were a novelty, that after such long travel and so many changes of scene you have not been able to shake off the gloom and heaviness of your mind? You need a change of soul rather than a change of climate. Though you may cross vast spaces of sea, and though, as our Virgil remarks, "Lands and cities are left astern," your faults will follow you whithersoever you travel.

LUCIUS SENECA, *LETTERS FROM A STOIC*, "XXVIII. ON TRAVEL AS A CURE FOR DISCONTENT" (FROM C. 63-65 CE)

If you have received the impression of any pleasure, guard yourself against being carried away by it; but let the thing wait for you, and allow yourself a certain delay on your own part. Then think of both times, of the time when you will enjoy the pleasure, and of the time after the enjoyment of the pleasure, when you will repent and will reproach yourself. And set against these things how you will rejoice, if you have abstained from the pleasure, and how you will commend yourself. But if it seems to you seasonable to undertake (do) the thing, take care that the charm of it, and the pleasure, and the attraction of it shall not conquer you; but set on the other side the consideration, how much better it is to be conscious that you have gained this victory.

EPICTETUS, *THE TEACHINGS OF A STOIC: SELECTED DISCOURSES AND THE ENCHIRIDION*, "THE MANUAL: XXXIV" (FROM C. EARLY 2ND CENTURY CE)

DETACHMENT

For though water, barley-meal, and crusts of barley-bread, are not a cheerful diet, yet it is the highest kind of Pleasure to be able to derive pleasure from this sort of food, and to have reduced one's needs to that modicum which no unfairness of Fortune can snatch away. Even prison fare is more generous; and those who have been set apart for capital punishment are not so meanly fed by the man who is to execute them. Therefore, what a noble soul must one have, to descend of one's own free will to a diet which even those who have been sentenced to death have not to fear! This is indeed forestalling the spear thrusts of Fortune.

LUCIUS SENECA, *LETTERS FROM A STOIC*, "XVIII. ON FESTIVALS AND FASTING" (FROM C. 63-65 CE)

ACCEPTANCE

Seek not that the things which happen should happen as you wish; but wish the things which happen to be as they are, and you will have a tranquil flow of life.

EPICTETUS, *THE TEACHINGS OF A STOIC: SELECTED DISCOURSES AND THE ENCHIRIDION*, "THE MANUAL: VIII" (FROM C. EARLY 2ND CENTURY CE)

CHANGE

172

You wander hither and yon, to rid yourself of the burden
that rests upon you, though it becomes more troublesome
by reason of your very restlessness, just as in a ship the cargo
when stationary makes no trouble, but when it shifts to this
side or that, it causes the vessel to heel more quickly in the
direction where it has settled. Anything you do tells against
you, and you hurt yourself by your very unrest; for you
are shaking up a sick man.

LUCIUS SENECA, *LETTERS FROM A STOIC*, "XXVIII. ON TRAVEL
AS A CURE FOR DISCONTENT" (FROM C. 63-65 CE)

ACCEPTANCE

173

What does it matter how much a man has laid up in his safe,
or in his warehouse, how large are his flocks and how fat his
dividends, if he covets his neighbour's property, and reckons,
not his past gains, but his hopes of gains to come? Do you
ask what is the proper limit to wealth? It is, first, to have
what is necessary, and, second, to have what is enough.

LUCIUS SENECA, *LETTERS FROM A STOIC*, "II. ON
DISCURSIVENESS IN READING" (FROM C. 63-65 CE)

So also in man we ought not to value the material, the poor flesh, but the principal (leading) things. What are these? Engaging in public business, marrying, begetting children, venerating God, taking care of parents, and generally, having desires, aversions, pursuits of things and avoidances, in the way in which we ought to do these things, and according to our nature. And how are we constituted by nature? Free, noble, modest; for what other animal blushes? What other is capable of receiving the appearance (the impression) of shame? And we are so constituted by nature as to subject pleasure to these things, as a minister, a servant, in order that it may call forth our activity, in order that it may keep us constant in acts which are conformable to nature.

EPICTETUS, *THE TEACHINGS OF A STOIC: SELECTED DISCOURSES AND THE ENCHIRIDION*, "TO THE ADMINISTRATOR OF THE FREE CITIES WHO WAS AN EPICUREAN" (FROM C. EARLY 2ND CENTURY CE)

CHANGE

175

...they are in a state of flux, constantly diminishing or increasing. None of us is the same man in old age that he was in youth; nor the same on the morrow as on the day preceding. Our bodies are burned along like flowing waters; every visible object accompanies time in its flight; of the things which we see, nothing is fixed. Even I myself as I comment on this change, am changed myself. This is just what Heraclitus says: "We go down twice into the same river, and yet into a different river." For the stream still keeps the same name, but the water has already flowed past. Of course this is much more evident in rivers than in human beings. Still, we mortals are also carried past in no less speedy a course; and this prompts me to marvel at our madness in cleaving with great affection to such a fleeting thing as the body, and in fearing lest some day we may die, when every instant means the death of our previous condition. Will you not stop fearing lest that may happen once which really happens every day? So much for man – a substance that flows away and falls, exposed to every influence; but the universe, too, immortal and enduring as it is, changes and never remains the same. For though it has within itself all that it has had, it has it in a different way from that in which it has had it; it keeps changing its arrangement.

LUCIUS SENECA, *LETTERS FROM A STOIC*, "LVIII. ON BEING" (FROM C. 63-65 CE)

CHANGE

Kindly remember that he whom you call your slave sprang from the same stock, is smiled upon by the same skies, and on equal terms with yourself breathes, lives, and dies. It is just as possible for you to see in him a free-born man as for him to see in you a slave... Despise, then, if you dare, those to whose estate you may at any time descend, even when you are despising them.

LUCIUS SENECA, *LETTERS FROM A STOIC*, "XLVII. ON MASTER AND SLAVE" (FROM C. 63-65 CE)

DETACHMENT

It is not possible that what is by nature free can be disturbed by anything else, or hindered by any other thing than by itself. But it is a man's own opinions which disturb him. For when the tyrant says to a man, I will chain your leg, he who values his leg says, Do not; have pity. But he who values his own will says, If it appears more advantageous to you, chain it. Do you not care? I do not care. I will show you that I am master.

EPICTETUS, *THE TEACHINGS OF A STOIC: SELECTED DISCOURSES AND THE ENCHIRIDION*, "HOW WE SHOULD BEHAVE TO TYRANTS" (FROM C. EARLY 2ND CENTURY CE)

NOBILITY OF THOUGHT

178

In one respect man is the nearest thing to me, so far as I must do good to men and endure them. But so far as some men make themselves obstacles to my proper acts, man becomes to me one of the things which are indifferent, no less than the sun or wind or a wild beast. Now it is true that these may impede my action, but they are no impediments to my affects and disposition, which have the power of acting conditionally and changing: for the mind converts and changes every hindrance to its activity into an aid; and so that which is a hindrance is made a furtherance to an act; and that which is an obstacle on the road helps us on this road.

MARCUS AURELIUS, *MEDITATIONS*, "BOOK V" (FROM C. 180 CE)

GOODNESS

179

For the ruling principle of a bad man cannot be trusted; it is insecure, has no certain rule by which it is directed, and is overpowered at different times by different appearances.

EPICTETUS, *THE TEACHINGS OF A STOIC: SELECTED DISCOURSES AND THE ENCHIRIDION*, "ON FRIENDSHIP" (FROM C. EARLY 2ND CENTURY CE)

When a soul rises superior to other souls, when it is under control, when it passes through every experience as if it were of small account, when it smiles at our fears and at our prayers, it is stirred by a force from heaven. A thing like this cannot stand upright unless it be propped by the divine. Therefore, a greater part of it abides in that place from whence it came down to earth. Just as the rays of the sun do indeed touch the earth, but still abide at the source from which they are sent; even so the great and hallowed soul, which has come down in order that we may have a nearer knowledge of divinity, does indeed associate with us, but still cleaves to its origin; on that source it depends, thither it turns its gaze and strives to go, and it concerns itself with our doings only as a being superior to ourselves.

LUCIUS SENECA, *LETTERS FROM A STOIC*, "XLI. ON THE GOD WITHIN US" (FROM C. 63-65 CE)

"Think on death", or rather, if you prefer the phrase, on "migration to heaven". The meaning is clear – that it is a wonderful thing to learn thoroughly how to die. You may deem it superfluous to learn a text that can be used only once; but that is just the reason why we ought to think on a thing. When we can never prove whether we really know a thing, we must always be learning it. "Think on death." In saying this, he bids us think on freedom. He who has learned to die has unlearned slavery; he is above any external power, or, at any rate, he is beyond it. What terrors have prisons and bonds and bars for him? His way out is clear. There is only one chain which binds us to life, and that is the love of life. The chain may not be cast off, but it may be rubbed away, so that, when necessity shall demand, nothing may retard or hinder us from being ready to do at once that which at some time we are bound to do.

LUCIUS SENECA, *LETTERS FROM A STOIC*, "XXVII. ON OLD AGE AND DEATH" (FROM C. 63-65 CE)

GOODNESS

Reverence that which is best in the universe; and this is that which makes use of all things and directs all things. And in like manner also reverence that which is best in thyself; and this is of the same kind as that. For in thyself also, that which makes use of everything else, is this, and thy life is directed by this.

MARCUS AURELIUS, *MEDITATIONS*, "BOOK V" (FROM C. 180 CE)

VIRTUE

"The knowledge of sin is the beginning of salvation." This saying of Epicurus seems to me to be a noble one. For he who does not know that he has sinned does not desire correction; you must discover yourself in the wrong before you can reform yourself. Some boast of their faults. Do you think that the man has any thought of mending his ways who counts over his vices as if they were virtues? Therefore, as far as possible, prove yourself guilty, hunt up charges against yourself; play the part, first of accuser, then of judge, last of intercessor. At times be harsh with yourself.

LUCIUS SENECA, *LETTERS FROM A STOIC*, "XXVIII. ON TRAVEL AS A CURE FOR DISCONTENT" (FROM C. 63-65 CE)

WILL

But what is philosophizing? Is it not a preparation against events which may happen?… If we give up philosophy, what shall we gain? What then should a man say on the occasion of each painful thing? It was for this that I exercised myself, for this I disciplined myself. God says to you: Give me a proof that you have duly practised athletics, that you have eaten what you ought, that you have been exercised… Then do you show yourself weak when the time for action comes? Now is the time for the fever. Let it be borne well. Now is the time for thirst, bear it well. Now is the time for hunger, bear it well. Is it not in your power? Who shall hinder you? The physician will hinder you from drinking; but he cannot prevent you from bearing thirst well: and he will hinder you from eating; but he cannot prevent you from bearing hunger well.

EPICTETUS, *THE TEACHINGS OF A STOIC: SELECTED DISCOURSES AND THE ENCHIRIDION*, "IN WHAT MANNER WE OUGHT TO BEAR SICKNESS" (FROM C. EARLY 2ND CENTURY CE)

VIRTUE

Count your years, and you will be ashamed to desire and pursue the same things you desired in your boyhood days. Of this one thing make sure against your dying day – let your faults die before you die. Away with those disordered pleasures, which must be dearly paid for; it is not only those which are to come that harm me, but also those which have come and gone. Just as crimes, even if they have not been detected when they were committed, do not allow anxiety to end with them; so with guilty pleasures, regret remains even after the pleasures are over. They are not substantial, they are not trustworthy; even if they do not harm us, they are fleeting. Cast about rather for some good which will abide. But there can be no such good except as the soul discovers it for itself within itself. Virtue alone affords everlasting and peace-giving joy; even if some obstacle arise, it is but like an intervening cloud, which floats beneath the sun but never prevails against it.

LUCIUS SENECA, *LETTERS FROM A STOIC*, "XXVII. ON THE GOOD WHICH ABIDES" (FROM C. 63-65 CE)

TIME

Often think of the rapidity with which things pass by and disappear, both the things which are and the things which are produced. For substance is like a river in a continual flow, and the activities of things are in constant change, and the causes work in infinite varieties; and there is hardly anything which stands still. And consider this which is near to thee, this boundless abyss of the past and of the future in which all things disappear. How then is he not a fool who is puffed up with such things or plagued about them and makes himself miserable? For they vex him only for a time, and a short time. Think of the universal substance, of which thou hast a very small portion; and of universal time, of which a short and indivisible interval has been assigned to thee; and of that which is fixed by destiny, and how small a part of it thou art.

MARCUS AURELIUS, *MEDITATIONS*, "BOOK V" (FROM C. 180 CE)

VIRTUE

187

"He is a slave." His soul, however, may be that of a freeman. "He is a slave." But shall that stand in his way? Show me a man who is not a slave; one is a slave to lust, another to greed, another to ambition, and all men are slaves to fear. I will name you an ex-consul who is slave to an old hag, a millionaire who is slave to a serving-maid; I will show you youths of the noblest birth in serfdom to pantomime players! No servitude is more disgraceful than that which is self-imposed.

LUCIUS SENECA, *LETTERS FROM A STOIC*, "XLVII. ON MASTER AND SLAVE" (FROM C. 63-65 CE)

CHANGE

188

Let us be brave in the face of hazards. Let us not fear wrongs, or wounds, or bonds, or poverty. And what is death? It is either the end, or a process of change. I have no fear of ceasing to exist; it is the same as not having begun. Nor do I shrink from changing into another state, because I shall, under no conditions, be as cramped as I am now.

LUCIUS SENECA, *LETTERS FROM A STOIC*, "LXV ON THE FIRST CAUSE" (FROM C. 63-65 CE)

COOPERATION WITH NATURE

189

But I cannot attend to my philosophical studies. And for what purpose do you follow them? Slave, is it not that you may be happy, that you may be constant, is it not that you may be in a state conformable to nature and live so? What hinders you when you have a fever from having your ruling faculty conformable to nature? Here is the proof of the thing, here is the test of the philosopher... What is it to bear a fever well? Not to blame God or man; not to be afflicted at that which happens, to expect death well and nobly, to do what must be done...

EPICTETUS, *THE TEACHINGS OF A STOIC: SELECTED DISCOURSES AND THE ENCHIRIDION*, "IN WHAT MANNER WE OUGHT TO BEAR SICKNESS" (FROM C. EARLY 2ND CENTURY CE)

DETACHMENT

190

Return to thy sober senses and call thyself back; and when thou hast roused thyself from sleep and hast perceived that they were only dreams which troubled thee, now in thy waking hours look at these [the things about thee] as thou didst look at those [the dreams].

MARCUS AURELIUS, *MEDITATIONS*, "BOOK VI" (FROM C. 180 CE)

WILL

Theophrastus, in his comparison of bad acts – such a comparison as one would make in accordance with the common notions of mankind – says, like a true philosopher, that the offences which are committed through desire are more blameable than those which are committed through anger. For he who is excited by anger seems to turn away from reason with a certain pain and unconscious contraction; but he who offends through desire, being overpowered by pleasure, seems to be in a manner more intemperate… in his offences. Rightly then, and in a way worthy of philosophy, he said that the offence which is committed with pleasure is more blameable than that which is committed with pain; and on the whole the one is more like a person who has been first wronged and through pain is compelled to be angry; but the other is moved by his own impulse to do wrong, being carried towards doing something by desire.

MARCUS AURELIUS, *MEDITATIONS*, "BOOK II" (FROM C. 180 CE)

DETACHMENT

For they do not understand how a man passes his life when he is alone, because they set out from a certain natural principle, from the natural desire of community and mutual love and from the pleasure of conversation among men. But nonetheless a man ought to be prepared in a manner for this also (being alone), to be able to be sufficient for himself and to be his own companion. For as Zeus dwells with himself, and is tranquil by himself, and thinks of his own administration and of its nature, and is employed in thoughts suitable to himself; so ought we also to be able to talk with ourselves, not to feel the want of others also, not to be unprovided with the means of passing our time; to observe the divine administration, and the relation of ourselves to everything else; to consider how we formerly were affected towards things that happened and how at present; what are still the things which give us pain; how these also can be cured and how removed; if any things require improvement, to improve them according to reason.

EPICTETUS, *THE TEACHINGS OF A STOIC: SELECTED DISCOURSES AND THE ENCHIRIDION*, "WHAT SOLITUDE IS, AND WHAT KIND OF PERSON A SOLITARY MAN IS" (FROM C. EARLY 2ND CENTURY CE)

WISDOM

193

…this is the surest proof which a man can get of his own constancy, if he neither seeks the things which are seductive and allure him to luxury, nor is led into them. It shows much more courage to remain dry and sober when the mob is drunk and vomiting; but it shows greater self-control to refuse to withdraw oneself and to do what the crowd does, but in a different way – thus neither making oneself conspicuous nor becoming one of the crowd. For one may keep holiday without extravagance.

LUCIUS SENECA, *LETTERS FROM A STOIC*, "XVIII. ON FESTIVALS AND FASTING" (FROM C. 63-65 CE)

DETACHMENT

194

If then you desire (aim at) such great things remember that you must not (attempt to) lay hold of them with a small effort; but you must leave alone some things entirely, and postpone others for the present.

EPICTETUS, *THE TEACHINGS OF A STOIC: SELECTED DISCOURSES AND THE ENCHIRIDION*, "THE MANUAL: I" (FROM C. EARLY 2ND CENTURY CE)

DETACHMENT

195

Let the part of thy soul which leads and governs be undisturbed by the movements in the flesh, whether of pleasure or of pain; and let it not unite with them, but let it circumscribe itself and limit those affects to their parts. But when these affects rise up to the mind by virtue of that other sympathy that naturally exists in a body which is all one, then thou must not strive to resist the sensation, for it is natural: but let not the ruling part of itself add to the sensation the opinion that it is either good or bad.

MARCUS AURELIUS, *MEDITATIONS*, "BOOK V" (FROM C. 180 CE)

VIRTUE

196

…we must cautiously enter into such intimacies with those of the common sort, and remember that it is impossible that a man can keep company with one who is covered with soot without being partaker of the soot himself.

EPICTETUS, *THE TEACHINGS OF A STOIC: SELECTED DISCOURSES AND THE ENCHIRIDION*, "THAT WE OUGHT WITH CAUTION TO ENTER INTO FAMILIAR INTERCOURSE WITH MEN" (FROM C. EARLY 2ND CENTURY CE)

GOODNESS

Solitude is a certain condition of a helpless man. For because
a man is alone, he is not for that reason also solitary; just as
though a man is among numbers, he is not therefore not
solitary. When then we have lost either a brother, or a son,
or a friend on whom we were accustomed to repose, we
say that we are left solitary, though we are often in Rome,
though such a crowd meet us, though so many live in the
same place… For the man who is solitary, as it is conceived,
is considered to be a helpless person and exposed to those
who wish to harm him. For this reason when we travel, then
especially do we say that we are lonely when we fall among
robbers, for it is not the sight of a human creature which
removes us from solitude, but the sight of one who is faithful
and modest and helpful to us…

EPICTETUS, *THE TEACHINGS OF A STOIC: SELECTED
DISCOURSES AND THE ENCHIRIDION*, "WHAT SOLITUDE IS,
AND WHAT KIND OF PERSON A SOLITARY MAN IS"
(FROM C. EARLY 2ND CENTURY CE)

VIRTUE

198

The person you are matters more than the place to which you go; for that reason we should not make the mind a bondsman to any one place. Live in this belief: "I am not born for any one corner of the universe; this whole world is my country." If you saw this fact clearly, you would not be surprised at getting no benefit from the fresh scenes to which you roam each time through weariness of the old scenes. For the first would have pleased you in each case, had you believed it wholly yours. As it is, however, you are not journeying; you are drifting and being driven, only exchanging one place for another, although that which you seek – to live well – is found everywhere.

LUCIUS SENECA, *LETTERS FROM A STOIC*, "XXVIII. ON TRAVEL AS A CURE FOR DISCONTENT" (FROM C. 63-65 CE)

CHANGE

199

Nature which governs the whole will soon change all things which thou seest, and out of their substance will make other things, and again other things from the substance of them…

MARCUS AURELIUS, *MEDITATIONS*, "BOOK VII" (FROM C. 180 CE)

GOODNESS

200

Art thou angry with him whose armpits stink? Art thou angry with him whose mouth smells foul? What good will this danger do thee? He has such a mouth, he has such armpits: it is necessary that such an emanation must come from such things – but the man has reason, it will be said, and he is able, if he takes pain, to discover wherein he offends – I wish thee well of thy discovery. Well then, and thou hast reason: by thy rational faculty stir up his rational faculty; show him his error, admonish him. For if he listens, thou wilt cure him, and there is no need of anger.

MARCUS AURELIUS, *MEDITATIONS*, "BOOK V" (FROM C. 180 CE)

WILL

201

Death is a cessation of the impressions through the senses, and of the pulling of the strings which move the appetites, and of the discursive movements of the thoughts, and of the service to the flesh. It is a shame for the soul to be first to give way in this life, when thy body does not give way.

MARCUS AURELIUS, *MEDITATIONS*, "BOOK VI" (FROM C. 180 CE)

GOODNESS

202

But he need never lack friends, for it lies in his own control
how soon he shall make good a loss… If you ask how
one can make oneself a friend quickly, I will tell you…
Hecato says: "…if you would be loved, love." Now there is
great pleasure, not only in maintaining old and established
friendships, but also in beginning and acquiring new ones.
There is the same difference between winning a new friend
and having already won him, as there is between the farmer
who sows and the farmer who reaps. The philosopher Attalus
used to say: "It is more pleasant to make than to keep a
friend, as it is more pleasant to the artist to paint than
to have finished painting."

LUCIUS SENECA, *LETTERS FROM A STOIC*, "IX. ON PHILOSOPHY
AND FRIENDSHIP" (FROM C. 63-65 CE)

GOODNESS

203

Whatever anyone does or says, I must be good, just as if the
gold, or the emerald, or the purple were always saying this.
I must be emerald and keep my colour.

MARCUS AURELIUS, *MEDITATIONS*, "BOOK VII" (FROM C. 180 CE)

COOPERATION WITH NATURE

Natural desires are limited; but those which spring from false opinion can have no stopping-point. The false has no limits. When you are travelling on a road, there must be an end; but when astray, your wanderings are limitless. Recall your steps, therefore, from idle things, and when you would know whether that which you seek is based upon a natural or upon a misleading desire, consider whether it can stop at any definite point. If you find, after having travelled far, that there is a more distant goal always in view, you may be sure that this condition is contrary to nature.

LUCIUS SENECA, *LETTERS FROM A STOIC*, "XVI. ON PHILOSOPHY, THE GUIDE OF LIFE" (FROM C. 63-65 CE)

COOPERATION WITH NATURE

Always run to the short way; and the short way is the natural: accordingly say and do everything in conformity with the soundest reason. For such a purpose frees a man from trouble, and warfare, and all artifice and ostentatious display.

MARCUS AURELIUS, *MEDITATIONS*, "BOOK IV" (FROM C. 180 CE)

If you bear a fever well, you have all that belongs to a man in a fever. What is it to bear a fever well? Not to blame God or man; not to be afflicted at that which happens, to expect death well and nobly, to do what must be done: when the physician comes in, not to be frightened at what he says; nor if he says you are doing well, to be overjoyed. For what good has he told you? And when you were in health, what good was that to you? And even if he says you are in a bad way, do not despond. For what is it to be ill? Is it that you are near the severance of the soul and the body? What harm is there in this? If you are not near now, will you not afterwards be near? Is the world going to be turned upside down when you are dead?

EPICTETUS, *THE TEACHINGS OF A STOIC: SELECTED DISCOURSES AND THE ENCHIRIDION*, "IN WHAT MANNER WE OUGHT TO BEAR SICKNESS" (FROM C. EARLY 2ND CENTURY CE)

VIRTUE

207

And call to recollection both how many things thou hast
passed through, and how many things thou hast been able
to endure: and that the history of thy life is now complete
and thy service is ended: and how many beautiful things
thou hast seen: and how many pleasures and pains thou hast
despised; and how many things called honourable thou hast
spurned; and to how many ill-minded folks thou hast
shown a kind disposition.

MARCUS AURELIUS, *MEDITATIONS*, "BOOK V" (FROM C. 180 CE)

CHANGE

208

Every great power (faculty) is dangerous to beginners.
You must then bear such things as you are able, but
conformably to nature… Practise sometimes a way
of living like a person out of health that you may at
some time live like a man in health.

EPICTETUS, *THE TEACHINGS OF A STOIC: SELECTED
DISCOURSES AND THE ENCHIRIDION*, "WHAT SOLITUDE IS,
AND WHAT KIND OF PERSON A SOLITARY MAN IS"
(FROM C. EARLY 2ND CENTURY CE)

CHANGE

As bad tragic actors cannot sing alone, but in company with many, so some persons cannot walk about alone. Man, if you are anything, both walk alone and talk to yourself, and do not hide yourself in the chorus. Examine a little at last, look around, stir yourself up, that you may know who you are.

EPICTETUS, *THE TEACHINGS OF A STOIC: SELECTED DISCOURSES AND THE ENCHIRIDION*, "WHAT SOLITUDE IS, AND WHAT KIND OF PERSON A SOLITARY MAN IS" (FROM C. EARLY 2ND CENTURY CE)

NOBILITY OF THOUGHT

The place where one lives, however, can contribute little towards tranquillity; it is the mind which must make everything agreeable to itself. I have seen men despondent in a gay and lovely villa, and I have seen them to all appearance full of business in the midst of a solitude. For this reason you should not refuse to believe that your life is well-placed merely because you are not now in Campania.

LUCIUS SENECA, *LETTERS FROM A STOIC*, "LV. ON VATIA'S VILLA" (FROM C. 63-65 CE)

VIRTUE

211

You must root out of men these two things, arrogance (pride) and distrust. Arrogance then is the opinion that you want nothing (are deficient in nothing); but distrust is the opinion that you cannot be happy when so many circumstances surround you. Arrogance is removed by confutation; and Socrates was the first who practised this. And (to know) that the thing is not impossible inquire and seek. This search will do you no harm; and in a manner this is philosophizing, to seek how it is possible to employ desire and aversion without impediment.

EPICTETUS, *THE TEACHINGS OF A STOIC: SELECTED DISCOURSES AND THE ENCHIRIDION*, "CERTAIN MISCELLANEOUS MATTERS" (FROM C. EARLY 2ND CENTURY CE)

CHANGE

212

Canst thou be nourished, unless the food undergoes a change? … Dost thou not see then that for thyself also to change is just the same, and equally necessary for the universal nature?

MARCUS AURELIUS, *MEDITATIONS*, "BOOK VII" (FROM C. 180 CE)

GOODNESS

…the same thing is advantageous to me which is advantageous to you; for I am not your friend unless whatever is at issue concerning you is my concern also. Friendship produces between us a partnership in all our interests. There is no such thing as good or bad fortune for the individual; we live in common. And no one can live happily who has regard to himself alone and transforms everything into a question of his own utility; you must live for your neighbour, if you would live for yourself. This fellowship, maintained with scrupulous care, which makes us mingle as men with our fellow-men and holds that the human race have certain rights in common, is also of great help in cherishing the more intimate fellowship which is based on friendship, concerning which I began to speak above. For he that has much in common with a fellow-man will have all things in common with a friend.

LUCIUS SENECA, *LETTERS FROM A STOIC*, "XLVIII. ON QUIBBLING AS UNWORTHY OF THE PHILOSOPHER" (FROM C. 63-65 CE)

This is the true athlete, the man who exercises himself against such appearances… Great is the combat, divine is the work; it is for kingship, for freedom, for happiness, for freedom from perturbation. Remember God; call on him as a helper and protector, as men at sea call on the Dioscuri in a storm. For what is a greater storm than that which comes from appearances which are violent and drive away the reason? For the storm itself, what else is it but an appearance? For take away the fear of death, and suppose as many thunders and lightnings as you please, and you will know what calm and serenity there is in the ruling faculty.

EPICTETUS, *THE TEACHINGS OF A STOIC: SELECTED DISCOURSES AND THE ENCHIRIDION*, "HOW WE SHOULD STRUGGLE AGAINST APPEARANCES" (FROM C. EARLY 2ND CENTURY CE)

ACCEPTANCE

Why then dost thou not wait in tranquility for thy end, whether it is extinction or removal to another state? And until that time comes, what is sufficient? Why, what else than to venerate the gods and bless them, and to do good to men, and to practise tolerance and self-restraint; but as to everything which is beyond the limits of the poor flesh and breath, to remember that this is neither thine nor in thy power. Thou canst pass thy life in an equable flow of happiness, if thou canst go by the right way, and think and act in the right way. These two things are common both to the soul of God and to the soul of man, and to the soul of every rational being, not to be hindered by another; and to hold good to consist in the disposition to justice and the practice of it, and in this to let thy desire find its termination.

MARCUS AURELIUS, *MEDITATIONS*, "BOOK V" (FROM C. 180 CE)

COOPERATION WITH NATURE

Men are stretching out imploring hands to you on all sides; lives ruined and in danger of ruin are begging for some assistance; men's hopes, men's resources, depend upon you. They ask that you deliver them from all their restlessness, that you reveal to them, scattered and wandering as they are, the clear light of truth. Tell them what nature has made necessary, and what superfluous; tell them how simple are the laws that she has laid down, how pleasant and unimpeded life is for those who follow these laws, but how bitter and perplexed it is for those who have put their trust in opinion rather than in nature.

LUCIUS SENECA, *LETTERS FROM A STOIC*, "XLVIII. ON QUIBBLING AS UNWORTHY OF THE PHILOSOPHER" (FROM C. 63-65 CE)

WISDOM

…restlessness is the sign of a disordered spirit. The primary indication, to my thinking, of a well ordered mind is a man's ability to remain in one place and linger in his own company.

LUCIUS SENECA, *LETTERS FROM A STOIC*, "II. ON DISCURSIVENESS IN READING" (FROM C. 63-65 CE)

This also is a saying of Epicurus: "If you live according to nature, you will never be poor; if you live according to opinion, you will never be rich." Nature's wants are slight; the demands of opinion are boundless. Suppose that the property of many millionaires is heaped up in your possession. Assume that fortune carries you far beyond the limits of a private income, decks you with gold, clothes you in purple, and brings you to such a degree of luxury and wealth that you can bury the earth under your marble floors; that you may not only possess, but tread upon, riches. Add statues, paintings, and whatever any art has devised for the luxury; you will only learn from such things to crave still greater.

LUCIUS SENECA, *LETTERS FROM A STOIC*, "XVI. ON PHILOSOPHY, THE GUIDE OF LIFE" (FROM C. 63-65 CE)

TIME

219

Frankness, and simplicity beseem true goodness. Even if there were many years left to you, you would have had to spend them frugally in order to have enough for the necessary things; but as it is, when your time is so scant, what madness it is to learn superfluous things!

LUCIUS SENECA, *LETTERS FROM A STOIC*, "XLVIII. ON QUIBBLING AS UNWORTHY OF THE PHILOSOPHER" (FROM C. 63-65 CE)

DETACHMENT

220

These reasonings do not cohere: I am richer than you, therefore I am better than you; I am more eloquent than you, therefore I am better than you. On the contrary, these rather cohere: I am richer than you, therefore my possessions are greater than yours; I am more eloquent than you, therefore my speech is superior to yours. But you are neither possession nor speech.

EPICTETUS, *THE TEACHINGS OF A STOIC: SELECTED DISCOURSES AND THE ENCHIRIDION*, "THE MANUAL: XLII" (FROM C. EARLY 2ND CENTURY CE)

ACCEPTANCE

You should come to him and say: Epictetus, we can no longer endure being bound to this poor body, and feeding it, and giving it drink and rest, and cleaning it, and for the sake of the body complying with the wishes of these and of those. Are not these things indifferent and nothing to us; and is not death no evil? And are we not in a manner kinsmen of God, and did we not come from him? Allow us to depart to the place from which we came; allow us to be released at last from these bonds by which we are bound and weighed down... And I on my part would say: Friends, wait for God: when he shall give the signal and release you from this service, then go to him; but for the present endure to dwell in this place where he has put you. Short indeed is this time of your dwelling here, and easy to bear for those who are so disposed; for what tyrant, or what thief, or what courts of justice are formidable to those who have thus considered as things of no value the body and the possessions of the body? Wait then, do not depart without a reason.

EPICTETUS, *THE TEACHINGS OF A STOIC: SELECTED DISCOURSES AND THE ENCHIRIDION*, "HOW FROM THE FACT THAT WE ARE AKIN TO GOD A MAN MAY PROCEED TO THE CONSEQUENCES" (FROM C. EARLY 2ND CENTURY CE)

COOPERATION WITH NATURE

If a man should be able to assent to this doctrine as he ought, that we are all sprung from God in an especial manner, and that God is the father both of men and of gods, I suppose that he would never have any ignoble or mean thoughts about himself… Yet we do not so; but since these two things are mingled in the generation of man, body in common with the animals, and reason and intelligence in common with the gods, many incline to this kinship, which is miserable and mortal; and some few to that which is divine and happy.

EPICTETUS, *THE TEACHINGS OF A STOIC: SELECTED DISCOURSES AND THE ENCHIRIDION*, "HOW A MAN SHOULD PROCEED FROM THE PRINCIPLE OF GOD BEING THE FATHER OF ALL MEN TO THE REST" (FROM C. EARLY 2ND CENTURY CE)

TIME

Everything material soon disappears in the substance of the whole; and everything formal [causal] is very soon taken back into the universal reason; and the memory of everything is very soon overwhelmed in time.

MARCUS AURELIUS, *MEDITATIONS*, "BOOK VII" (FROM C. 180 CE)

COOPERATION WITH NATURE

The substance of the universe is obedient and compliant; and the reason which governs it has in itself no cause for doing evil, for it has no malice, nor does it do evil to anything, nor is anything harmed by it. But all things are made and perfected according to this reason.

MARCUS AURELIUS, *MEDITATIONS*, "BOOK VI" (FROM C. 180 CE)

CHANGE

"But," you say, "it is the greatest possible disadvantage to be worn out and to die off, or rather, if I may speak literally, to melt away! For we are not suddenly smitten and laid low; we are worn away, and every day reduces our powers to a certain extent." But is there any better end to it all than to glide off to one's proper haven, when nature slips the cable? Not that there is anything painful in a shock and a sudden departure from existence; it is merely because this other way of departure is easy – a gradual withdrawal.

LUCIUS SENECA, *LETTERS FROM A STOIC*, "XXVII. ON OLD AGE AND DEATH" (FROM C. 63-65 CE)

NOBILITY OF THOUGHT

Men are disturbed not by the things which happen, but by the opinions about the things; for example, death is nothing terrible, for if it were it would have seemed so to Socrates; for the opinion about death that it is terrible, is the terrible thing. When then we are impeded, or disturbed, or grieved, let us never blame others, but ourselves – that is, our opinions. It is the act of an ill-instructed man to blame others for his own bad condition; it is the act of one who has begun to be instructed, to lay the blame on himself; and of one whose instruction is completed, neither to blame another, nor himself.

EPICTETUS, *THE TEACHINGS OF A STOIC: SELECTED DISCOURSES AND THE ENCHIRIDION*, "THE MANUAL: V" (FROM C. EARLY 2ND CENTURY CE)

VIRTUE

Thou wilt soon die, and thou art not yet simple, not free from perturbations, nor without suspicion of being hurt by external things, nor kindly disposed towards all; nor dost thou yet place wisdom only in acting justly.

MARCUS AURELIUS, *MEDITATIONS*, "BOOK IV" (FROM C. 180 CE)

Examine yourself; scrutinize and observe yourself in diverse ways; but mark, before all else, whether it is in philosophy or merely in life itself that you have made progress. Philosophy is no trick to catch the public; it is not devised for show. It is a matter, not of words, but of facts. It is not pursued in order that the day may yield some amusement before it is spent, or that our leisure may be relieved of a tedium that irks us. It moulds and constructs the soul; it orders our life, guides our conduct, shows us what we should do and what we should leave undone; it sits at the helm and directs our course as we waver amid uncertainties. Without it, no one can live fearlessly or in peace of mind. Countless things that happen every hour call for advice; and such advice is to be sought in philosophy.

LUCIUS SENECA, *LETTERS FROM A STOIC*, "XVI. ON PHILOSOPHY, THE GUIDE OF LIFE" (FROM C. 63-65 CE)

DETACHMENT

229

He who has a vehement desire for posthumous fame does not consider that every one of those who remember him will himself also die very soon; then again also they who have succeeded them, until the whole remembrance shall have been extinguished as it is transmitted through men who foolishly admire and perish. But suppose that those who will remember are even immortal, and that the remembrance will be immortal, what then is this to thee? And I say not what is it to the dead, but what is it to the living? What is praise except indeed so far as it has a certain utility? For thou now rejectest unseasonably the gift of nature, clinging to something else...

MARCUS AURELIUS, *MEDITATIONS*, "BOOK IV" (FROM C. 180 CE)

COOPERATION WITH NATURE

230

Everything harmonizes with me, which is harmonious to thee, O Universe. Nothing for me is too early nor too late, which is in due time for thee. Everything is fruit to me which thy seasons bring, O Nature: from thee are all things, in thee are all things, to thee all things return.

MARCUS AURELIUS, *MEDITATIONS*, "BOOK IV" (FROM C. 180 CE)

CHANGE

I am composed of the formal and the material; and neither of them will perish into nonexistence, as neither of them came into existence out of nonexistence. Every part of me then will be reduced by change into some part of the universe, and that again will change into another part of the universe, and so on forever. And by consequence of such a change I too exist, and those who begot me, and so on forever in the other direction.

MARCUS AURELIUS, *MEDITATIONS*, "BOOK V" (FROM C. 180 CE)

COOPERATION WITH NATURE

In the morning when thou risest unwillingly, let this thought be present – I am rising to the work of a human being. Why then am I dissatisfied if I am going to do the things for which I exist and for which I was brought into the world? Or have I been made for this, to lie in the bedclothes and keep myself warm? But this is more pleasant. Dost thou exist then to take thy pleasure, and not at all for action or exertion?

MARCUS AURELIUS, *MEDITATIONS*, "BOOK V" (FROM C. 180 CE)

Just as fire cannot be crushed out, since it will escape round the edges of the body which overwhelms it; just as the air cannot be damaged by lashes and blows, or even cut into, but flows back about the object to which it gives place; similarly the soul, which consists of the subtlest particles, cannot be arrested or destroyed inside the body, but, by virtue of its delicate substance, it will rather escape through the very object by which it is being crushed. Just as lightning, no matter how widely it strikes and flashes, makes its return through a narrow opening, so the soul, which is still subtler than fire, has a way of escape through any part of the body. We therefore come to this question – whether the soul can be immortal. But be sure of this: if the soul survives the body after the body is crushed, the soul can in no wise be crushed out, precisely because it does not perish; for the rule of immortality never admits of exceptions, and nothing can harm that which is everlasting.

LUCIUS SENECA, *LETTERS FROM A STOIC*, "LVII.
ON TRIALS OF TRAVEL" (FROM C. 63-65 CE)

NOBILITY OF THOUGHT

Do you ask what will be the difference between yourself and the gods? They will live longer. But, by my faith, it is the sign of a great artist to have confined a full likeness to the limits of a miniature. The wise man's life spreads out to him over as large a surface as does all eternity to a god. There is one point in which the sage has an advantage over the god; for a god is freed from terrors by the bounty of nature, the wise man by his own bounty. What a wonderful privilege, to have the weaknesses of a man and the serenity of a god! The power of philosophy to blunt the blows of chance is beyond belief.

LUCIUS SENECA, *LETTERS FROM A STOIC*, "LIII. ON THE FAULTS OF THE SPIRIT" (FROM C. 63-65 CE)

COOPERATION WITH NATURE

Consider thyself to be dead, and to have completed thy life up to the present time; and live according to nature the remainder which is allowed thee.

MARCUS AURELIUS, *MEDITATIONS*, "BOOK VII" (FROM C. 180 CE)

Try how the life of the good man suits thee, the life of him who is satisfied with his portion out of the whole, and satisfied with his own just acts and benevolent disposition.

Hast thou seen those things? Look also at these. Do not disturb thyself. Make thyself all simplicity. Does anyone do wrong? It is to himself that he does the wrong. Has anything happened to thee? Well; out of the universe from the beginning everything which happens has been apportioned and spun out to thee. In a word, thy life is short. Thou must turn to profit the present by the aid of reason and justice. Be sober in thy relaxation. Either it is a well-arranged universe or a chaos huddled together, but still a universe. But can a certain order subsist in thee, and disorder in the All?

MARCUS AURELIUS, *MEDITATIONS*, "BOOK IV" (FROM C. 180 CE)

There is this difference between ourselves and the other school: our ideal wise man feels his troubles, but overcomes them; their wise man does not even feel them. But we and they alike hold this idea – that the wise man is self-sufficient. Nevertheless, he desires friends, neighbours, and associates, no matter how much he is sufficient unto himself. And mark how self-sufficient he is; for on occasion he can be content with a part of himself. If he lose a hand through disease or war, or if some accident puts out one or both of his eyes, he will be satisfied with what is left, taking as much pleasure in his impaired and maimed body as he took when it was sound. But while he does not pine for these parts if they are missing, he prefers not to lose them. In this sense the wise man is self-sufficient, that he can do without friends, not that he desires to do without them. When I say "can", I mean this: he endures the loss of a friend with equanimity.

LUCIUS SENECA, *LETTERS FROM A STOIC*, "IX. ON PHILOSOPHY AND FRIENDSHIP" (FROM C. 63-65 CE)

As on a voyage when the vessel has reached a port, if you go out to get water it is an amusement by the way to pick up a shellfish or some bulb, but your thoughts ought to be directed to the ship, and you ought to be constantly watching if the captain should call, and then you must throw away all those things, that you may not be bound and pitched into the ship like sheep. So in life also, if there be given to you instead of a little bulb and a shell a wife and child, there will be nothing to prevent (you from taking them). But if the captain should call, run to the ship and leave all those things without regard to them. But if you are old, do not even go far from the ship, lest when you are called you make default.

EPICTETUS, *THE TEACHINGS OF A STOIC: SELECTED DISCOURSES AND THE ENCHIRIDION*, "THE MANUAL: VII" (FROM C. EARLY 2ND CENTURY CE)

For what purpose, then, do I make a man my friend? In order to have someone for whom I may die, whom I may follow into exile, against whose death I may stake my own life, and pay the pledge, too. The friendship which you portray is a bargain and not a friendship; it regards convenience only, and looks to the results. Beyond question the feeling of a lover has in it something akin to friendship; one might call it friendship run mad. But, though this is true, does anyone love for the sake of gain, or promotion, or renown? Pure love, careless of all other things, kindles the soul with desire for the beautiful object, not without the hope of a return of the affection. What then? Can a cause which is more honourable produce a passion that is base? You may retort: "We are now discussing the question whether friendship is to be cultivated for its own sake." On the contrary, nothing more urgently requires demonstration; for if friendship is to be sought for its own sake, he may seek it who is self-sufficient. "How, then," you ask, "does he seek it?" Precisely as he seeks an object of great beauty, not attracted to it by desire for gain, nor yet frightened by the instability of Fortune. One who seeks friendship for favourable occasions, strips it of all its nobility.

LUCIUS SENECA, *LETTERS FROM A STOIC*, "IX. ON PHILOSOPHY AND FRIENDSHIP" (FROM C. 63–65 CE)

Pleasure… Subject it to the rule, throw it into the balance. Ought the good to be such a thing that it is fit that we have confidence in it? Yes. And in which we ought to confide? It ought to be. Is it fit to trust to anything which is insecure? No. Is then pleasure anything secure? No. Take it then and throw it out of the scale, and drive it far away from the place of good things. But if you are not sharp sighted, and one balance is not enough for you, bring another. Is it fit to be elated over what is good? Yes. Is it proper then to be elated over present pleasure? … Thus things are tested and weighed when the rules are ready. And to philosophize is this, to examine and confirm the rules; and then to use them when they are known is the act of a wise and good man.

EPICTETUS, *THE TEACHINGS OF A STOIC: SELECTED DISCOURSES AND THE ENCHIRIDION*, "WHAT THE BEGINNING OF PHILOSOPHY IS" (FROM C. EARLY 2ND CENTURY CE)

CHANGE

Observe constantly that all things take place by change, and accustom thyself to consider that the nature of the Universe loves nothing so much as to change the things which are and to make new things like them. For everything that exists is in a manner the seed of that which will be.

MARCUS AURELIUS, *MEDITATIONS*, "BOOK IV" (FROM C. 180 CE)

COOPERATION WITH NATURE

In every act observe the things which come first, and those which follow it; and so proceed to the act. If you do not, at first you will approach it with alacrity, without having thought of the things which will follow… My man, first of all consider what kind of thing it is; and then examine your own nature, if you are able to sustain the character. Do you wish to be a pentathlete or a wrestler? Look at your arms, your thighs, examine your loins. For different men are formed by nature for different things…

EPICTETUS, *THE TEACHINGS OF A STOIC: SELECTED DISCOURSES AND THE ENCHIRIDION*, "THE MANUAL: XXIX" (FROM C. EARLY 2ND CENTURY CE)

243

"Cherish some man of high character, and keep him ever before your eyes, living as if he were watching you, and ordering all your actions as if he beheld them." ... We can get rid of most sins, if we have a witness who stands near us when we are likely to go wrong. The soul should have someone whom it can respect – one by whose authority it may make even its inner shrine more hallowed. Happy is the man who can make others better, not merely when he is in their company, but even when he is in their thoughts! And happy also is he who can so revere a man as to calm and regulate himself by calling him to mind! One who can so revere another, will soon be himself worthy of reverence... Choose a master whose life, conversation, and soul expressing face have satisfied you; picture him always to yourself as your protector or your pattern. For we must indeed have someone according to whom we may regulate our characters; you can never straighten that which is crooked unless you use a ruler.

LUCIUS SENECA, *LETTERS FROM A STOIC*, "XI. ON THE BLUSH OF MODESTY" (FROM C. 63-65 CE)

Of things some are in our power, and others are not. In our power are opinion, movement towards a thing, desire, aversion, turning from a thing; and in a word, whatever are our acts. Not in our power are the body, property, reputation, offices (magisterial power), and in a word, whatever are not our own acts. And the things in our power are by nature free, not subject to restraint or hindrance; but the things not in our power are weak, slavish, subject to restraint, in the power of others. Remember then, that if you think the things which are by nature slavish to be free, and the things which are in the power of others to be your own, you will be hindered, you will lament, you will be disturbed, you will blame both gods and men; but if you think that only which is your own to be your own, and if you think that what is another's, as it really is, belongs to another, no man will ever compel you, no man will hinder you, you will never blame any man, you will accuse no man, you will do nothing involuntarily (against your will), no man will harm you, you will have no enemy, for you will not suffer any harm.

EPICTETUS, *THE TEACHINGS OF A STOIC: SELECTED DISCOURSES AND THE ENCHIRIDION*, "THE MANUAL: I" (FROM C. EARLY 2ND CENTURY CE)

VIRTUE

No man ought to glory except in that which is his own.
We praise a vine if it makes the shoots teem with increase,
if by its weight it bends to the ground the very poles which
hold its fruit; would any man prefer to this vine one from
which golden grapes and golden leaves hang down? In a
vine the virtue peculiarly its own is fertility; in man also we
should praise that which is his own… Praise the quality in
him which cannot be given or snatched away, that which
is the peculiar property of the man. Do you ask what this
is? It is soul, and reason brought to perfection in the soul.
For man is a reasoning animal. Therefore, man's highest
good is attained, if he has fulfilled the good for which nature
designed him at birth. And what is it which this reason
demands of him? The easiest thing in the world – to live
in accordance with his own nature. But this is turned into
a hard task by the general madness of mankind; we push
one another into vice. And how can a man be recalled to
salvation, when he has none to restrain him, and all
mankind to urge him on?

LUCIUS SENECA, *LETTERS FROM A STOIC*, "XLI.
ON THE GOD WITHIN US" (FROM C. 63-65 CE)

GOODNESS

But my nature is rational and social; and my city and country, so far as I am Antoninus, is Rome, but so far as I am a man, it is the world. The things then which are useful to these cities are alone useful to me. Whatever happens to every man, this is for the interest of the universal: this might be sufficient. But further thou wilt observe this also as a general truth, if thou dost observe, that whatever is profitable to any man is profitable also to other men. But let the word profitable be taken here in the common sense as said of things of the middle kind, neither good nor bad.

MARCUS AURELIUS, *MEDITATIONS*, "BOOK VI" (FROM C. 180 CE)

DETACHMENT

…there is no bitterness in doing without that which you have ceased to desire. Moreover, every pain sometimes stops, or at any rate slackens; moreover, one may take precautions against its return, and, when it threatens, may check it by means of remedies.

LUCIUS SENECA, *LETTERS FROM A STOIC*, "LXXVIII. ON THE HEALING POWER OF THE MIND" (FROM C. 63-65 CE)

ACCEPTANCE

248

...he whom you love is mortal, and that what you love is nothing of your own; it has been given to you for the present, not that it should not be taken from you, nor has it been given to you for all time, but as a fig is given to you or a bunch of grapes at the appointed season of the year.

EPICTETUS, *THE TEACHINGS OF A STOIC: SELECTED DISCOURSES AND THE ENCHIRIDION*, "THE MANUAL: L" (FROM C. EARLY 2ND CENTURY CE)

TIME

249

What soul then has skill and knowledge? That which knows beginning and end, and knows the reason which pervades all substance and through all time by fixed periods [revolutions] administers the universe. Soon, very soon, thou wilt be ashes, or a skeleton, and either a name or not even a name; but name is sound and echo.

MARCUS AURELIUS, *MEDITATIONS*, "BOOK V" (FROM C. 180 CE)

250

Whatever things (rules) are proposed to you (for the conduct of life) abide by them, as if they were laws, as if you would be guilty of impiety if you transgressed any of them. And whatever any man shall say about you, do not attend to it; for this is no affair of yours. How long will you then still defer thinking yourself worthy of the best things, and in no matter transgressing the distinctive reason? Have you accepted the theorems (rules), which it was your duty to agree to, and have you agreed to them? What teacher then do you still expect that you defer to him the correction of yourself? You are no longer a youth, but already a full-grown man.

EPICTETUS, *THE TEACHINGS OF A STOIC: SELECTED DISCOURSES AND THE ENCHIRIDION*, "THE MANUAL: L" (FROM C. EARLY 2ND CENTURY CE)

Thou wilt see all these things, people marrying, bringing up children, sick, dying, warring, feasting, trafficking, cultivating the ground, flattering, obstinately arrogant, suspecting, plotting, wishing for some to die, grumbling about the present, loving, heaping up treasure, desiring consulship, kingly power. Well then, that life of these people no longer exists at all. In like manner view also the other epochs of time and of whole nations, and see how many after great efforts soon fell and were resolved into the elements. But chiefly thou shouldst think of those whom thou hast thyself known distracting themselves about idle things, neglecting to do what was in accordance with their proper constitution, and to hold firmly to this and to be content with it. And herein it is necessary to remember that the attention given to everything has its proper value and proportion. For thus thou wilt not be dissatisfied, if thou appliest thyself to smaller matters no further than is fit.

MARCUS AURELIUS, *MEDITATIONS*, "BOOK IV" (FROM C. 180 CE)

WILL

You must be one man either good or bad; you must either labor at your own ruling faculty or at external things; you must either labor at things within or at external things; that is, you must either occupy the place of a philosopher or that of one of the vulgar.

EPICTETUS, *THE TEACHINGS OF A STOIC: SELECTED DISCOURSES AND THE ENCHIRIDION*, "THAT WE OUGHT TO PROCEED WITH CIRCUMSPECTION TO EVERYTHING" (FROM C. EARLY 2ND CENTURY CE)

NOBILITY OF THOUGHT

It is a dangerous habit also to approach obscene talk. When then, anything of this kind happens, if there is a good opportunity, rebuke the man who has proceeded to this talk; but if there is not an opportunity, by your silence at least, and blushing and expression of dissatisfaction by your countenance, show plainly that you are displeased at such talk.

EPICTETUS, *THE TEACHINGS OF A STOIC: SELECTED DISCOURSES AND THE ENCHIRIDION*, "THE MANUAL: XXXIII" (FROM C. EARLY 2ND CENTURY CE)

"'Twas night, and all the world was lulled to rest." This is not true; for no real rest can be found when reason has not done the lulling. Night brings our troubles to the light, rather than banishes them; it merely changes the form of our worries. For even when we seek slumber, our sleepless moments are as harassing as the daytime. Real tranquillity is the state reached by an unperverted mind when it is relaxed. Think of the unfortunate man who courts sleep by surrendering his spacious mansion to silence, who, that his ear may be disturbed by no sound, bids the whole retinue of his slaves be quiet and that whoever approaches him shall walk on tiptoe; he tosses from this side to that and seeks a fitful slumber amid his frettings! He complains that he has heard sounds, when he has not heard them at all. The reason, you ask? His soul's in an uproar; it must be soothed, and its rebellious murmuring checked. You need not suppose that the soul is at peace when the body is still. Sometimes quiet means disquiet.

LUCIUS SENECA, *LETTERS FROM A STOIC*, "LVI. ON QUIET AND STUDY" (FROM C. 63-65 CE)

TIME

255

For all things soon pass away and become a mere tale, and complete oblivion soon buries them. And I say this of those who have shone in a wondrous way. For the rest, as soon as they have breathed out their breath, they are gone, and no man speaks of them. And, to conclude the matter, what is even an eternal remembrance? A mere nothing. What then is that about which we ought to employ our serious pains? This one thing, thoughts just, and acts social, and words which never lie, and a disposition which gladly accepts all that happens, as necessary, as usual, as flowing from a principle and source of the same kind.

MARCUS AURELIUS, *MEDITATIONS*, "BOOK IV" (FROM C. 180 CE)

NOBILITY OF THOUGHT

256

Call to mind what honourable or brave deeds you have done; consider the good side of your own life. Run over in your memory those things which you have particularly admired.

LUCIUS SENECA, *LETTERS FROM A STOIC*, "LXXVIII. ON THE HEALING POWER OF THE MIND" (FROM C. 63-65 CE)

DETACHMENT

257

The mind which starts at words or at chance sounds is
unstable and has not yet withdrawn into itself; it contains
within itself an element of anxiety and rooted fear, and this
makes one a prey to care… You may therefore be sure that
you are at peace with yourself, when no noise readies you,
when no word shakes you out of yourself, whether it be
of flattery or of threat, or merely an empty sound buzzing
about you with unmeaning din.

LUCIUS SENECA, *LETTERS FROM A STOIC*, "LVI. ON QUIET
AND STUDY" (FROM C. 63-65 CE)

WILL

258

I often entertained the impulse of ending my life then and
there; but the thought of my kind old father kept me back.
For I reflected, not how bravely I had the power to die, but
how little power he had to bear bravely the loss of me.
And so I commanded myself to live. For sometimes it is
an act of bravery even to live.

LUCIUS SENECA, *LETTERS FROM A STOIC*, "LXXVIII. ON THE
HEALING POWER OF THE MIND" (FROM C. 63-65 CE)

259

There is only one way to happiness, and let this rule be ready both in the morning and during the day and by night: the rule is not to look towards things which are out of the power of our will, to think that nothing is our own, to give up all things to the Divinity, to Fortune… for a man to observe that only which is his own, that which cannot be hindered; and when we read, to refer our reading to this only, and our writing and our listening. For never commend a man on account of these things which are common to all, but on account of his opinions (principles); for these are the things which belong to each man, which make his actions bad or good.

EPICTETUS, *THE TEACHINGS OF A STOIC: SELECTED DISCOURSES AND THE ENCHIRIDION*, "TO THOSE WHO ARE DESIROUS OF PASSING LIFE IN TRANQUILITY" (FROM C. EARLY 2ND CENTURY CE)

If you were ill, you would stop caring for your personal concerns, and forget your business duties; you would not think highly enough of any client to take active charge of his case during a slight abatement of your sufferings. You would try your hardest to be rid of the illness as soon as possible. What, then? Shall you not do the same thing now? Throw aside all hindrances and give up your time to getting a sound mind; for no man can attain it if he is engrossed in other matters. Philosophy wields her own authority; she appoints her own time and does not allow it to be appointed for her. She is not a thing to be followed at odd times, but a subject for daily practice; she is mistress, and she commands our attendance.

LUCIUS SENECA, *LETTERS FROM A STOIC*, "LIII. ON THE FAULTS OF THE SPIRIT" (FROM C. 63-65 CE)

Well then God constitutes every animal, one to be eaten, another to serve for agriculture, another to supply cheese, and another for some like use; for which purposes what need is there to understand appearances and to be able to distinguish them? But God has introduced man to be a spectator of God and of his works; and not only a spectator of them, but an interpreter. For this reason it is shameful for man to begin and to end where irrational animals do; but rather he ought to begin where they begin, and to end where nature ends in us; and nature ends in contemplation and understanding, and in a way of life conformable to nature. Take care then not to die without having been spectators of these things.

EPICTETUS, *THE TEACHINGS OF A STOIC: SELECTED DISCOURSES AND THE ENCHIRIDION, "OF PROVIDENCE"* (FROM C. EARLY 2ND CENTURY CE)

DETACHMENT

262

Occupy thyself with few things, says the philosopher, if thou wouldst be tranquil – But consider if it would not be better to say, Do what is necessary, and whatever the reason of the animal which is naturally social requires, and as it requires. For this brings not only the tranquility which comes from doing well, but also that which comes from doing few things. For the greatest part of what we say and do being unnecessary, if a man takes this away, he will have more leisure and less uneasiness. Accordingly on every occasion a man should ask himself, Is this one of the unnecessary things? Now a man should take away not only unnecessary acts, but also, unnecessary thoughts, for thus superfluous acts will not follow after.

MARCUS AURELIUS, *MEDITATIONS*, "BOOK IV" (FROM C. 180 CE)

NOBILITY OF THOUGHT

263

If a thing is difficult to be accomplished by thyself, do not think that it is impossible for man: but if anything is possible for man and conformable to his nature, think that this can be attained by thyself too.

MARCUS AURELIUS, *MEDITATIONS*, "BOOK VI" (FROM C. 180 CE)

Then after receiving everything from another and even yourself, are you angry and do you blame the giver if he takes anything from you? Who are you, and for what purpose did you come into the world? Did not he (God) introduce you here, did he not show you the light, did he not give you fellow-workers, and perceptions and reason? And as whom did he introduce you here? Did he not introduce you as subject to death, and as one to live on the Earth with a little flesh, and to observe his administration, and to join with him in the spectacle and the festival for a short time? Will you not then, as long as you have been permitted, after seeing the spectacle and the solemnity, when he leads you out, go with adoration of him and thanks for what you have heard and seen? ... For what purpose then have I received these things? To use them. How long? So long as he who has lent them chooses. What if they are necessary to me? Do not attach yourself to them and they will not be necessary; do not say to yourself that they are necessary, and then they are not necessary.

EPICTETUS, *THE TEACHINGS OF A STOIC: SELECTED DISCOURSES AND THE ENCHIRIDION*, "TO THOSE WHO FALL OFF (DESIST) FROM THEIR PURPOSE" (FROM C. EARLY 2ND CENTURY CE)

But you will reply: "What pleasure do you get from wasting your time on these problems, which relieve you of none of your emotions, route none of your desires?" So far as I am concerned, I treat and discuss them as matters which contribute greatly toward calming the spirit, and I search myself first, and then the world about me. And not even now am I, as you think, wasting my time. For all these questions, provided that they be not chopped up and torn apart into such unprofitable refinements, elevate and lighten the soul, which is weighted down by a heavy burden and desires to be freed and to return to the elements of which it was once a part. For this body of ours is a weight upon the soul and its penance; as the load presses down the soul is crushed and is in bondage, unless philosophy has come to its assistance and has bid it take fresh courage by contemplating the universe, and has turned it from things earthly to things divine. There it has its liberty, there it can roam abroad; meantime it escapes the custody in which it is bound, and renews its life in heaven.

LUCIUS SENECA, *LETTERS FROM A STOIC*, "LXV. ON THE FIRST CAUSE" (FROM C. 63-65 CE)

DETACHMENT

I consist of a little body and a soul. Now to this little body all things are indifferent, for it is not able to perceive differences. But to the understanding those things only are indifferent, which are not the works of its own activity. But whatever things are the works of its own activity, all these are in its power. And of these however only those which are done with reference to the present; for as to the future and the past activities of the mind, even these are for the present indifferent.

MARCUS AURELIUS, *MEDITATIONS*, "BOOK VI" (FROM C. 180 CE)

CHANGE

We see that the carpenter when he has learned certain things becomes a carpenter; the pilot by learning certain things becomes a pilot. May it not then in philosophy also not be sufficient to wish to be wise and good, and that there is also a necessity to learn certain things? We inquire then what these things are.

EPICTETUS, *THE TEACHINGS OF A STOIC: SELECTED DISCOURSES AND THE ENCHIRIDION*, "TO NASO" (FROM C. EARLY 2ND CENTURY CE)

ACCEPTANCE

There is no sorrow in the world, when we have escaped from the fear of death. There are these three serious elements in every disease: fear of death, bodily pain, and interruption of pleasures. Concerning death enough has been said, and I shall add only a word: this fear is not a fear of disease, but a fear of nature. Disease has often postponed death, and a vision of dying has been many a man's salvation. You will die, not because you are ill, but because you are alive; even when you have been cured, the same end awaits you; when you have recovered, it will be not death, but ill-health, that you have escaped.

LUCIUS SENECA, *LETTERS FROM A STOIC*, "LXXVIII. ON THE HEALING POWER OF THE MIND" (FROM C. 63-65 CE)

COOPERATION WITH NATURE

All things are implicated with one another, and the bond is holy; there is hardly anything unconnected with any other thing. For things have been coordinated, and they combine to form the same universe [order].

MARCUS AURELIUS, *MEDITATIONS*, "BOOK VII" (FROM C. 180 CE)

What then is the punishment of those who do not accept?
It is to be what they are. Is any person dissatisfied with
being alone? Let him be alone. Is a man dissatisfied with his
parents? Let him be a bad son, and lament. Is he dissatisfied
with his children? Let him be a bad father. Cast him into
prison. What prison? Where he is already, for he is there
against his will; and where a man is against his will, there he
is in prison. So Socrates was not in prison, for he was there
willingly. Must my leg then be lamed? Wretch, do you then
on account of one poor leg find fault with the world? Will
you not willingly surrender it for the whole? Will you
not withdraw from it? Will you not gladly part with it
to him who gave it?

EPICTETUS, *THE TEACHINGS OF A STOIC: SELECTED
DISCOURSES AND THE ENCHIRIDION*, "OF PROVIDENCE"
(FROM C. EARLY 2ND CENTURY CE)

WISDOM

271

What is the first business of him who philosophizes? To throw away self-conceit. For it is impossible for a man to begin to learn that which he thinks that he knows. As to things then which ought to be done and ought not to be done, and good and bad, and beautiful and ugly, all of us talking of them at random go to the philosophers; and on these matters we praise, we censure, we accuse, we blame, we judge and determine about principles honorable and dishonorable. But why do we go to the philosophers? Because we wish to learn what we do not think that we know.

EPICTETUS, *THE TEACHINGS OF A STOIC: SELECTED DISCOURSES AND THE ENCHIRIDION*, "THAT WE DO NOT STRIVE TO USE OUR OPINIONS ABOUT GOOD AND EVIL" (FROM C. EARLY 2ND CENTURY CE)

DETACHMENT

272

Think not so much of what thou hast not as of what thou hast: but of the things which thou hast select the best, and then reflect how eagerly they would have been sought, if thou hadst them not.

MARCUS AURELIUS, *MEDITATIONS*, "BOOK VII" (FROM C. 180 CE)

We are weak, watery beings standing in the midst of unrealities; therefore let us turn our minds to the things that are everlasting. Let us look up to the ideal outlines of all things, that flit about on high, and to the God who moves among them and plans how he may defend from death that which he could not make imperishable because its substance forbade, and so by reason may overcome the defects of the body. For all things abide, not because they are everlasting, but because they are protected by the care of him who governs all things; but that which was imperishable would need no guardian. The Master Builder keeps them safe, overcoming the weakness of their fabric by his own power.

LUCIUS SENECA, *LETTERS FROM A STOIC*, "LVIII. ON BEING" (FROM C. 63-65 CE)

If a man possesses any superiority, or thinks that he does when he does not, such a man, if he is uninstructed, will of necessity be puffed up through it. For instance, the tyrant says, I am master of all! And what can you do for me? Can you give me desire which shall have no hindrance? How can you? Have you the infallible power of avoiding what you would avoid? Have you the power of moving towards an object without error? And how do you possess this power? Come, when you are in a ship, do you trust to yourself or to the helmsman? And when you are in a chariot, to whom do you trust but to the driver? And how is it in all other arts? Just the same.

EPICTETUS, *THE TEACHINGS OF A STOIC: SELECTED DISCOURSES AND THE ENCHIRIDION*, "HOW WE SHOULD BEHAVE TO TYRANTS" (FROM C. EARLY 2ND CENTURY CE)

DETACHMENT

Keep by every means what is your own; do not desire what belongs to others. Fidelity (integrity) is your own, virtuous shame is your own; who then can take these things from you? Who else than yourself will hinder you from using them? But how do you act? When you seek what is not your own, you lose that which is your own.

EPICTETUS, *THE TEACHINGS OF A STOIC: SELECTED DISCOURSES AND THE ENCHIRIDION*, "HOW WE SHOULD STRUGGLE WITH CIRCUMSTANCES" (FROM C. EARLY 2ND CENTURY CE)

COOPERATION WITH NATURE

One man after burying another has been laid out dead, and another buries him: and all this in a short time. To conclude, always observe how ephemeral and worthless human things are, and what was yesterday a little mucus tomorrow will be a mummy or ashes. Pass then through this little space of time conformably to nature, and end thy journey in content, just as an olive falls off when it is ripe, blessing nature who produced it, and thanking the tree on which it grew.

MARCUS AURELIUS, *MEDITATIONS*, "BOOK IV" (FROM C. 180 CE)

DETACHMENT

277

Why then are we angry? Is it because we value so much the things of which these men rob us? Do not admire your clothes, and then you will not be angry with the thief. Consider this matter thus: you have fine clothes; your neighbour has not; you have a window; you wish to air the clothes. The thief does not know wherein man's good consists, but he thinks that it consists in having fine clothes, the very thing which you also think. Must he not then come and take them away? When you show a cake to greedy persons, and swallow it all yourself, do you expect them not to snatch it from you? Do not provoke them…

EPICTETUS, *THE TEACHINGS OF A STOIC: SELECTED DISCOURSES AND THE ENCHIRIDION*, "THAT WE OUGHT NOT TO BE ANGRY WITH THE ERRORS (FAULTS) OF OTHERS" (FROM C. EARLY 2ND CENTURY CE)

TIME

278

Let not future things disturb thee, for thou wilt come to them, if it shall be necessary, having with thee the same reason which now thou usest for present things.

MARCUS AURELIUS, *MEDITATIONS*, "BOOK VII" (FROM C. 180 CE)

CHANGE

Man, consider first what the matter is (which you propose to do), then your own nature also, what it is able to bear. If you are a wrestler, look at your shoulders, your thighs, your loins: for different men are naturally formed for different things. Do you think that, if you do (what you are doing daily), you can be a philosopher? Do you think that you can eat as you do now, drink as you do now, and in the same way be angry and out of humour? You must watch, labour, conquer certain desires… When you have considered all these things completely, then, if you think proper, approach to philosophy, if you would gain in exchange for these things freedom from perturbations, liberty, tranquillity.

EPICTETUS, *THE TEACHINGS OF A STOIC: SELECTED DISCOURSES AND THE ENCHIRIDION*, "THAT WE OUGHT TO PROCEED WITH CIRCUMSPECTION TO EVERYTHING" (FROM C. EARLY 2ND CENTURY CE)

VIRTUE

The young character, which cannot hold fast to righteousness, must be rescued from the mob; it is too easy to side with the majority. Even Socrates, Cato, and Laelius might have been shaken in their moral strength by a crowd that was unlike them; so true it is that none of us, no matter how much he cultivates his abilities, can withstand the shock of faults that approach, as it were, with so great a retinue. Much harm is done by a single case of indulgence or greed; the familiar friend, if he be luxurious, weakens and softens us imperceptibly; the neighbour, if he be rich, rouses our covetousness; the companion, if he be slanderous, rubs off some of his rust upon us, even though we be spotless and sincere. What then do you think the effect will be on character, when the world at large assaults it! You must either imitate or loathe the world. But both courses are to be avoided; you should not copy the bad simply because they are many, nor should you hate the many because they are unlike you.

LUCIUS SENECA, *LETTERS FROM A STOIC*, "VII. ON CROWDS" (FROM C. 63-65 CE)

DETACHMENT

Be not elated at any advantage (excellence) which belongs to another. If a horse when he is elated should say, I am beautiful, one might endure it. But when you are elated, and say, I have a beautiful horse, you must know that you are elated at having a good horse. What then is your own? The use of appearances. Consequently when in the use of appearances you are conformable to nature, then be elated, for then you will be elated at something good which is your own.

EPICTETUS, *THE TEACHINGS OF A STOIC: SELECTED DISCOURSES AND THE ENCHIRIDION*, "THE MANUAL: VI" (FROM C. EARLY 2ND CENTURY CE)

COOPERATION WITH NATURE

Constantly regard the universe as one living being, having one substance and one soul; and observe how all things have reference to one perception, the perception of this one living being; and how all things act with one movement; and how all things are the cooperating causes of all things which exist; observe too the continuous spinning of the thread and the contexture of the web.

MARCUS AURELIUS, *MEDITATIONS*, "BOOK IV" (FROM C. 180 CE)

The wise man, I say, self-sufficient though he be,
nevertheless desires friends if only for the purpose of
practising friendship, in order that his noble qualities may
not lie dormant. Not, however, for the purpose mentioned
by Epicurus in the letter quoted above: "That there may be
someone to sit by him when he is ill, to help him when he
is in prison or in want"; but that he may have someone by
whose sick-bed he himself may sit, someone a prisoner in
hostile hands whom he himself may set free. He who regards
himself only, and enters upon friendships for this reason,
reckons wrongly. The end will be like the beginning: he has
made friends with one who might assist him out of bondage;
at the first rattle of the chain such a friend will desert him.

LUCIUS SENECA, *LETTERS FROM A STOIC*, "IX. ON PHILOSOPHY
AND FRIENDSHIP" (FROM C. 63-65 CE)

VIRTUE

This is the chief thing: Be not perturbed, for all things are according to the nature of the universal; and in a little time thou wilt be nobody and nowhere, like Hadrian and Augustus. In the next place having fixed thy eyes steadily on thy business look at it, and at the same time remembering that it is thy duty to be a good man, and what man's nature demands, do that without turning aside; and speak as it seems to thee most just, only let it be with a good disposition and with modesty and without hypocrisy.

MARCUS AURELIUS, *MEDITATIONS*, "BOOK VIII" (FROM C. 180 CE)

WILL

Set aside a certain number of days, during which you shall be content with the scantiest and cheapest fare, with coarse and rough dress, saying to yourself the while: "Is this the condition that I feared?" It is precisely in times of immunity from care that the soul should toughen itself beforehand for occasions of greater stress, and it is while Fortune is kind that it should fortify itself against her violence. In days of peace the soldier performs manoeuvres, throws up earthworks with no enemy in sight, and wearies himself by gratuitous toil, in order that he may be equal to unavoidable toil. If you would not have a man flinch when the crisis comes, train him before it comes.

LUCIUS SENECA, *LETTERS FROM A STOIC*, "XVIII. ON FESTIVALS AND FASTING" (FROM C. 63-65 CE)

You may hold converse with your friends when they are absent, and indeed as often as you wish and for as long as you wish. For we enjoy this, the greatest of pleasures, all the more when we are absent from one another. For the presence of friends makes us fastidious; and because we can at any time talk or sit together, when once we have parted we give not a thought to those whom we have just beheld. And we ought to bear the absence of friends cheerfully, just because everyone is bound to be often absent from his friends even when they are present. Include among such cases, in the first place, the nights spent apart, then the different engagements which each of two friends has, then the private studies of each and their excursions into the country, and you will see that foreign travel does not rob us of much.

LUCIUS SENECA, *LETTERS FROM A STOIC*, "LV. ON VATIA'S VILLA" (FROM C. 63-65 CE)

DETACHMENT

287

…how foolish we are to fear certain objects to a greater or less degree, since all of them end in the same way. For what difference does it make whether a watchtower or a mountain crashes down upon us? No difference at all, you will find. Nevertheless, there will be some men who fear the latter mishap to a greater degree, though both accidents are equally deadly; so true it is that fear looks not to the effect, but to the cause of the effect.

LUCIUS SENECA, *LETTERS FROM A STOIC*, "LVII. ON TRIALS OF TRAVEL" (FROM C. 63-65 CE)

ACCEPTANCE

288

Let it make no difference to thee whether thou art cold or warm, if thou art doing thy duty; and whether thou art drowsy or satisfied with sleep; and whether ill-spoken of or praised; and whether dying or doing something else. For it is one of the acts of life, this act by which we die: it is sufficient then in this act also to do well what we have in hand.

MARCUS AURELIUS, *MEDITATIONS*, "BOOK VI" (FROM C. 180 CE)

...they utter these useless words from their real opinions; but you utter your elegant words only from your lips; for this reason they are without strength and dead, and it is nauseous to listen to your exhortations and your miserable virtue, which is talked of everywhere (up and down). In this way the vulgar have the advantage over you; for every opinion is strong and invincible. Until then the good sentiments are fixed in you, and you shall have acquired a certain power for your security, I advise you to be careful in your association with common persons; if you are not, every day like wax in the sun there will be melted away whatever you inscribe on your minds in the school.

EPICTETUS, *THE TEACHINGS OF A STOIC: SELECTED DISCOURSES AND THE ENCHIRIDION*, "THAT WE OUGHT WITH CAUTION TO ENTER INTO FAMILIAR INTERCOURSE WITH MEN" (FROM C. EARLY 2ND CENTURY CE)

COOPERATION WITH NATURE

290

The universe is either a confusion, and a mutual involution of things, and a dispersion; or it is unity and order and providence. If then it is the former, why do I desire to tarry in a fortuitous combination of things and such a disorder? And why do I care about anything else than how I shall at last become earth? And why am I disturbed, for the dispersion of my elements will happen whatever I do. But if the other supposition is true, I venerate, and I am firm, and I trust in him who governs.

MARCUS AURELIUS, *MEDITATIONS*, "BOOK VI" (FROM C. 180 CE)

GOODNESS

291

When thou hast done a good act and another has received it, why dost thou look for a third thing besides these, as fools do, either to have the reputation of having done a good act or to obtain a return? No man is tired of receiving what is useful. But it is useful to act according to nature. Do not then be tired of receiving what is useful by doing it to others.

MARCUS AURELIUS, *MEDITATIONS*, "BOOK VII" (FROM C. 180 CE)

WILL

…this is the law of nature and of God that the superior shall always overpower the inferior. In what? In that in which it is superior. One body is stronger than another: many are stronger than one: the thief is stronger than he who is not a thief… a man has seized me by the cloak, and is drawing me to the public place: then others bawl out, Philosopher, what has been the use of your opinions? See, you are dragged to prison, you are going to be beheaded. And what system of philosophy could I have made so that, if a stronger man should have laid hold of my cloak, I should not be dragged off; that if ten men should have laid hold of me and cast me into prison, I should not be cast in? Have I learned nothing else then? I have learned to see that everything which happens, if it be independent of my will, is nothing to me.

EPICTETUS, *THE TEACHINGS OF A STOIC: SELECTED DISCOURSES AND THE ENCHIRIDION*, "ON CONSTANCY (OR FIRMNESS)" (FROM C. EARLY 2ND CENTURY CE)

VIRTUE

293

These are the so-called "fair-weather" friendships; one who is chosen for the sake of utility will be satisfactory only so long as he is useful. Hence prosperous men are blockaded by troops of friends; but those who have failed stand amid vast loneliness, their friends fleeing from the very crisis which is to test their worth.

LUCIUS SENECA, *LETTERS FROM A STOIC*, "IX. ON PHILOSOPHY AND FRIENDSHIP" (FROM C. 63-65 CE)

GOODNESS

294

For now who among us is not able to discourse according to the rules of art about good and evil things (in this fashion)? That of things some are good, and some are bad, and some are indifferent: the good then are virtues, and the things which participate in virtues; and the bad are the contrary; and the indifferent are wealth, health, reputation.

EPICTETUS, *THE TEACHINGS OF A STOIC: SELECTED DISCOURSES AND THE ENCHIRIDION*, "THAT WHEN WE CANNOT FULFIL THAT WHICH THE CHARACTER OF A MAN PROMISES, WE ASSUME THE CHARACTER OF A PHILOSOPHER" (FROM C. EARLY 2ND CENTURY CE)

The hypothetical proposition is indifferent: the judgment about it is not indifferent, but it is either knowledge or opinion or error. Thus life is indifferent: the use is not indifferent. When any man then tells you that these things also are indifferent, do not become negligent; and when a man invites you to be careful (about such things), do not become abject and struck with admiration of material things. And it is good for you to know your own preparation and power, that in those matters where you have not been prepared, you may keep quiet, and not be vexed, if others have the advantage over you. For you too in syllogisms will claim to have the advantage over them; and if others should be vexed at this, you will console them by saying, "I have learned them, and you have not." Thus also where there is need of any practice, seek not that which is acquired from the need (of such practice), but yield in that matter to those who have had practice, and be yourself content with firmness of mind.

EPICTETUS, *THE TEACHINGS OF A STOIC: SELECTED DISCOURSES AND THE ENCHIRIDION*, "OF INDIFFERENCE" (FROM C. EARLY 2ND CENTURY CE)

DETACHMENT

…where there are things which appear most worthy of our approbation, we ought to lay them bare and look at their worthlessness and strip them of all the words by which they are exalted. For outward show is a wonderful perverter of the reason, and when thou art most sure that thou art employed about things worth thy pains, it is then that it cheats thee most.

MARCUS AURELIUS, *MEDITATIONS*, "BOOK VI" (FROM C. 180 CE)

NOBILITY OF THOUGHT

Will you not then seek the nature of good in the rational animal? For if it is not there, you will not choose to say that it exists in any other thing (plant or animal). What then? Are not plants and animals also the works of God? They are; but they are not superior things, nor yet parts of the gods. But you are a superior thing; you are a portion separated from the Deity; you have in yourself a certain portion of him. Why then are you ignorant of your own noble descent?

EPICTETUS, *THE TEACHINGS OF A STOIC: SELECTED DISCOURSES AND THE ENCHIRIDION*, "HOW WE OUGHT TO USE DIVINATION" (FROM C. EARLY 2ND CENTURY CE)

298

Confidence (courage) then ought to be employed against death, and caution against the fear of death. But now we do the contrary, and employ against death the attempt to escape; and to our opinion about it we employ carelessness, rashness, and indifference. These things Socrates properly used to call tragic masks; for as to children masks appear terrible and fearful from inexperience, we also are affected in like manner by events (the things which happen in life) for no other reason than children are by masks. For what is a child? Ignorance. What is a child? Want of knowledge. For when a child knows these things, he is in no way inferior to us. What is death? A tragic mask. Turn it and examine it. See, it does not bite. The poor body must be separated from the spirit either now or later as it was separated from it before. Why then are you troubled if it be separated now? For if it is not separated now, it will be separated afterwards…

EPICTETUS, *THE TEACHINGS OF A STOIC: SELECTED DISCOURSES AND THE ENCHIRIDION*, "THAT CONFIDENCE (COURAGE) IS NOT INCONSISTENT WITH CAUTION)" (FROM C. EARLY 2ND CENTURY CE)

VIRTUE

Freedom. For in these matters we must not believe the many, who say that free persons only ought to be educated, but we should rather believe the philosophers who say that the educated only are free. How is this? In this manner: Is freedom anything else than the power of living as we choose? Nothing else. Tell me then, ye men, do you wish to live in error? We do not. No one then who lives in error is free. Do you wish to live in fear? Do you wish to live in sorrow? Do you wish to live in perturbation? By no means. No one then who is in a state of fear or sorrow or perturbation is free; but whoever is delivered from sorrows and fears and perturbations, he is at the same time also delivered from servitude… For philosophers say we allow none to be free except the educated; that is, God does not allow it.

EPICTETUS, *THE TEACHINGS OF A STOIC: SELECTED DISCOURSES AND THE ENCHIRIDION*, "THAT CONFIDENCE (COURAGE) IS NOT INCONSISTENT WITH CAUTION" (FROM C. EARLY 2ND CENTURY CE)

COOPERATION WITH NATURE

300

Every instrument, tool, vessel, if it does that for which it has been made, is well, and yet he who made it is not there. But in the things which are held together by nature there is within and there abides in them the power which made them; wherefore the more is it fit to reverence this power, and to think, that, if thou dost live and act according to its will, everything in thee is in conformity to intelligence. And thus also in the universe the things which belong to it are in conformity to intelligence.

MARCUS AURELIUS, *MEDITATIONS*, "BOOK VI" (FROM C. 180 CE)

DETACHMENT

301

Then examine it (things) by the rules which you possess, and by this first and chiefly, whether it relates to the things which are in our power or to things which are not in our power; and if it relates to anything which is not in our power, be ready to say that it does not concern you.

EPICTETUS, *THE TEACHINGS OF A STOIC: SELECTED DISCOURSES AND THE ENCHIRIDION*, "THE MANUAL: I" (FROM C. EARLY 2ND CENTURY CE)

COOPERATION WITH NATURE

Let us now return to the consideration of the characteristic disadvantage of disease: it is accompanied by great suffering. The suffering, however, is rendered endurable by interruptions; for the strain of extreme pain must come to an end. No man can suffer both severely and for a long time; Nature, who loves us most tenderly, has so constituted us as to make pain either endurable or short.

LUCIUS SENECA, *LETTERS FROM A STOIC*, "LXXVIII. ON THE HEALING POWER OF THE MIND" (FROM C. 63-65 CE)

DETACHMENT

Remember that not only the desire of power and of riches makes us mean and subject to others, but even the desire of tranquillity, and of leisure, and of travelling abroad, and of learning. For, to speak plainly, whatever the external thing may be, the value which we set upon it places us in subjection to others.

EPICTETUS, *THE TEACHINGS OF A STOIC: SELECTED DISCOURSES AND THE ENCHIRIDION*, "TO THOSE WHO FALL OFF (DESIST) FROM THEIR PURPOSE" (FROM C. EARLY 2ND CENTURY CE)

VIRTUE

I, at any rate, as if the test were at hand and the day were come which is to pronounce its decision concerning all the years of my life, watch over myself and commune thus with myself: "The showing which we have made up to the present time, in word or deed, counts for nothing. All this is but a trifling and deceitful pledge of our spirit, and is wrapped in much charlatanism. I shall leave it to Death to determine what progress I have made. Therefore with no faint heart I am making ready for the day when, putting aside all stage artifice and actor's rouge, I am to pass judgment upon myself – whether I am merely declaiming brave sentiments, or whether I really feel them; whether all the bold threats I have uttered against fortune are a pretence and a farce…"

LUCIUS SENECA, *LETTERS FROM A STOIC*, "XXVII. ON OLD AGE AND DEATH" (FROM C. 63-65 CE)

What are you? A man. If you consider yourself as detached from other men, it is according to nature to live to old age, to be rich, to be healthy. But if you consider yourself as a man and a part of a certain whole, it is for the sake of that whole that at one time you should be sick, at another time take a voyage and run into danger, and at another time be in want, and in some cases die prematurely. Why then are you troubled? Do you not know, that as a foot is no longer a foot if it is detached from the body, so you are no longer a man if you are separated from other men. For what is a man? A part of a state, of that first which consists of gods and of men; then of that which is called next to it, which is a small image of the universal state.

EPICTETUS, *THE TEACHINGS OF A STOIC: SELECTED DISCOURSES AND THE ENCHIRIDION*, "OF TRANQUILITY (FREEDOM FROM PERTURBATION)" (FROM C. EARLY 2ND CENTURY CE)

CHANGE

306

If souls continue to exist, how does the air contain them from eternity? But how does the earth contain the bodies of those who have been buried from time so remote? For as here the mutation of these bodies after a certain continuance, whatever it may be, and their dissolution make room for other dead bodies; so the souls which are removed into the air after subsisting for some time are transmuted and diffused, and assume a fiery nature by being received into the seminal intelligence of the universe, and in this way make room for the fresh souls which come to dwell there. And this is the answer which a man might give on the hypothesis of souls continuing to exist.

MARCUS AURELIUS, *MEDITATIONS*, "BOOK IV" (FROM C. 180 CE)

WISDOM

307

Wipe out the imagination. Stop the pulling of the strings. Confine thyself to the present. Understand well what happens either to thee or to another.

MARCUS AURELIUS, *MEDITATIONS*, "BOOK VII" (FROM C. 180 CE)

Perhaps someone will say: "How can philosophy help me, if Fate exists? Of what avail is philosophy, if God rules the universe? Of what avail is it, if Chance governs everything? For not only is it impossible to change things that are determined, but it is also impossible to plan beforehand against what is undetermined; either God has forestalled my plans, and decided what I am to do, or else Fortune gives no free play to my plans." Whether the truth, Lucilius, lies in one or in all of these views, we must be philosophers; whether Fate binds us down by an inexorable law, or whether God as arbiter of the universe has arranged everything, or whether Chance drives and tosses human affairs without method, philosophy ought to be our defence. She will encourage us to obey God cheerfully, but Fortune defiantly; she will teach us to follow God and endure Chance.

LUCIUS SENECA, *LETTERS FROM A STOIC*, "XVI. ON PHILOSOPHY, THE GUIDE OF LIFE" (FROM C. 63-65 CE)

Such is the course which those men have followed who, in their imitation of poverty, have every month come almost to want, that they might never recoil from what they had so often rehearsed... There is no reason, however, why you should think that you are doing anything great; for you will merely be doing what many thousands of slaves and many thousands of poor men are doing every day. But you may credit yourself with this item – that you will not be doing it under compulsion, and that it will be as easy for you to endure it permanently as to make the experiment from time to time... Let us become intimate with poverty, so that Fortune may not catch us off our guard. We shall be rich with all the more comfort, if we once learn how far poverty is from being a burden.

LUCIUS SENECA, *LETTERS FROM A STOIC*, "XVIII. ON FESTIVALS AND FASTING" (FROM C. 63-65 CE)

WISDOM

310

The wise man, the seeker after wisdom, is bound closely, indeed, to his body, but he is an absentee so far as his better self is concerned, and he concentrates his thoughts upon lofty things. Bound, so to speak, to his oath of allegiance, he regards the period of life as his term of service. He is so trained that he neither loves nor hates life; he endures a mortal lot, although he knows that an ampler lot is in store for him.

LUCIUS SENECA, *LETTERS FROM A STOIC*, "LXV ON THE FIRST CAUSE" (FROM C. 63-65 CE)

VIRTUE

311

In the mind of one who is chastened and purified thou wilt find no corrupt matter, nor impurity, nor any sore skinned over. Nor is his life incomplete when fate overtakes him, as one may say of an actor who leaves the stage before ending and finishing the play. Besides, there is in him nothing servile, nor affected, nor too closely bound to other things, nor yet detached from other things, nothing worthy of blame, nothing which seeks a hiding-place.

MARCUS AURELIUS, *MEDITATIONS*, "BOOK III" (FROM C. 180 CE)

So long as future things are uncertain, I always cling to those which are more adapted to the conservation of that which is according to nature; for God himself has given me the faculty of such choice. But if I knew that it was fated (in the order of things) for me to be sick, I would even move towards it… For why are ears of corn produced? Is it not that they may become dry? And do they not become dry that they may be reaped? For they are not separated from communion with other things. If then they had perception, ought they to wish never to be reaped? But this is a curse upon ears of corn to be never reaped. So we must know that in the case of men too it is a curse not to die, just the same as not to be ripened and not to be reaped. But since we must be reaped, and we also know that we are reaped, we are vexed at it; for we neither know what we are nor have we studied what belongs to man…

EPICTETUS, *THE TEACHINGS OF A STOIC: SELECTED DISCOURSES AND THE ENCHIRIDION*, "OF INDIFFERENCE" (FROM C. EARLY 2ND CENTURY CE)

CHANGE

Some things are hurrying into existence, and others are hurrying out of it; and of that which is coming into existence part is already extinguished. Motions and changes are continually renewing the world, just as the uninterrupted course of time is always renewing the infinite duration of ages. In this flowing stream then, on which there is no abiding, what is there of the things which hurry by on which a man would set a high price? It would be just as if a man should fall in love with one of the sparrows which fly by, but it has already passed out of sight. Something of this kind is the very life of every man, like the exhalation of the blood and the respiration of the air. For such as it is to have once drawn in the air and to have given it back, which we do every moment, just the same is it with the whole respiratory power, which thou didst receive at thy birth yesterday and the day before, to give it back to the element from which thou didst first draw it.

MARCUS AURELIUS, *MEDITATIONS*, "BOOK VI" (FROM C. 180 CE)

Do you forbid me to contemplate the universe? Do you compel me to withdraw from the whole and restrict me to a part? May I not ask what are the beginnings of all things, who moulded the universe, who took the confused and conglomerate mass of sluggish matter, and separated it into its parts? May I not inquire who is the Master-Builder of this universe, how the mighty bulk was brought under the control of law and order, who gathered together the scattered atoms, who separated the disordered elements and assigned an outward form to elements that lay in one vast shapelessness?… Am I not to ask these questions?

Must I be ignorant of the heights whence I have descended? Whether I am to see this world but once, or to be born many times? What is my destination afterwards? What abode awaits my soul on its release from the laws of slavery among men? Do you forbid me to have a share in heaven? In other words, do you bid me live with my head bowed down? No, I am above such an existence; I was born to a greater destiny than to be a mere chattel of my body, and I regard this body as nothing but a chain which manacles my freedom. Therefore, I offer it as a sort of buffer to fortune, and shall allow no wound to penetrate through to my soul. For my body is the only part of me which can suffer injury. In this dwelling, which is exposed to peril, my soul lives free.

LUCIUS SENECA, *LETTERS FROM A STOIC*, "LXV ON THE FIRST CAUSE" (FROM C. 63-65 CE)

VIRTUE

315

Such will I show myself to you, faithful, modest, noble, free from perturbation. What, and immortal, too, except from old age, and from sickness? No, but dying as becomes a god, sickening as becomes a god. This power I possess; this I can do. But the rest I do not possess, nor can I do. I will show the nerves (strength) of a philosopher. What nerves are these? A desire never disappointed, an aversion which never falls on that which it would avoid, a proper pursuit, a diligent purpose, an assent which is not rash. These you shall see.

EPICTETUS, *THE TEACHINGS OF A STOIC: SELECTED DISCOURSES AND THE ENCHIRIDION*, "HOW WE OUGHT TO USE DIVINATION" (FROM C. EARLY 2ND CENTURY CE)

COOPERATION WITH NATURE

What then is worth being valued? To be received with clapping of hands? No. Neither must we value the clapping of tongues, for the praise which comes from the many is a clapping of tongues. Suppose then that thou hast given up this worthless thing called fame, what remains that is worth valuing? This in my opinion, to move thyself and to restrain thyself in conformity to thy proper constitution, to which end both all employments and arts lead. For every art aims at this, that the thing which has been made should be adapted to the work for which it has been made; and both the vine-planter who looks after the vine, and the horse-breaker, and he who trains the dog, seek this end.

MARCUS AURELIUS, *MEDITATIONS*, "BOOK VI" (FROM C. 180 CE)

VIRTUE

Adorn thyself with simplicity and modesty and with indifference towards the things which lie between virtue and vice. Love mankind. Follow God. The poet says that Law rules all. And it is enough to remember that Law rules all.

MARCUS AURELIUS, *MEDITATIONS*, "BOOK VII" (FROM C. 180 CE)

WISDOM

318

…it is the unexpected that puts the heaviest load upon us. Strangeness adds to the weight of calamities, and every mortal feels the greater pain as a result of that which also brings surprise. Therefore, nothing ought to be unexpected by us. Our minds should be sent forward in advance to meet all problems, and we should consider, not what is wont to happen, but what can happen.

LUCIUS SENECA, *LETTERS FROM A STOIC*, "XCI. ON THE LESSON TO BE DRAWN FROM THE BURNING OF LYONS" (FROM C. 63-65 CE)

COOPERATION WITH NATURE

319

All things are made up of matter and of God; God controls matter, which encompasses him and follows him as its guide and leader. And that which creates, in other words, God, is more powerful and precious than matter, which is acted upon by God. God's place in the universe corresponds to the soul's relation to man. World-matter corresponds to our mortal body; therefore let the lower serve the higher.

LUCIUS SENECA, *LETTERS FROM A STOIC*, "LXV ON THE FIRST CAUSE" (FROM C. 63-65 CE)

VIRTUE

320

…modest actions preserve the modest man, and immodest actions destroy him; and actions of fidelity preserve the faithful man, and the contrary actions destroy him. And on the other hand contrary actions strengthen contrary characters: shamelessness strengthens the shameless man, faithlessness the faithless man, abusive words the abusive man, anger the man of an angry temper, and unequal receiving and giving make the avaricious man more avaricious. For this reason philosophers admonish us not to be satisfied with learning only, but also to add study, and then practice. For we have long been accustomed to do contrary things, and we put in practice opinions which are contrary to true opinions. If then we shall not also put in practice right opinions, we shall be nothing more than the expositors of the opinions of others.

EPICTETUS, *THE TEACHINGS OF A STOIC: SELECTED DISCOURSES AND THE ENCHIRIDION*, "THAT WHEN WE CANNOT FULFIL THAT WHICH THE CHARACTER OF A MAN PROMISES, WE ASSUME THE CHARACTER OF A PHILOSOPHER" (FROM C. EARLY 2ND CENTURY CE)

DETACHMENT

Wilt thou not cease to value many other things too?
Then thou wilt be neither free, nor sufficient for thy own
happiness, nor without passion. For of necessity thou
must be envious, jealous, and suspicious of those who can
take away those things, and plot against those who have
that which is valued by thee. Of necessity a man must be
altogether in a state of perturbation who wants any of these
things; and besides, he must often find fault with the gods.
But to reverence and honour thy own mind will make thee
content with thyself, and in harmony with society, and in
agreement with the gods, that is, praising all that they
give and have ordered.

MARCUS AURELIUS, *MEDITATIONS*, "BOOK VI" (FROM C. 180 CE)

VIRTUE

Many men praise you; but have you any reason for being
pleased with yourself, if you are a person whom the many
can understand? Your good qualities should face inwards.

LUCIUS SENECA, *LETTERS FROM A STOIC*, "VII. ON
CROWDS" (FROM C. 63-65 CE)

Consider who you are. In the first place, you are a man;
and this is one who has nothing superior to the faculty of
the will, but all other things subjected to it; and the faculty
itself he possesses unenslaved and free from subjection.
Consider then from what things you have been separated
by reason. You have been separated from wild beasts; you
have been separated from domestic animals. Further, you
are a citizen of the world, and a part of it, not one of the
subservient (serving), but one of the principal (ruling)
parts, for you are capable of comprehending the divine
administration and of considering the connection of
things. What then does the character of a citizen promise
(profess)? To hold nothing as profitable to himself; to
deliberate about nothing as if he were detached from the
community, but to act as the hand or foot would do, if
they had reason and understood the constitution of nature,
for they would never put themselves in motion nor desire
anything otherwise than with reference to the whole.

EPICTETUS, *THE TEACHINGS OF A STOIC: SELECTED
DISCOURSES AND THE ENCHIRIDION*, "HOW WE MAY
DISCOVER THE DUTIES OF LIFE FROM NAMES"
(FROM C. EARLY 2ND CENTURY CE)

Every habit and faculty is maintained and increased by the corresponding actions: the habit of walking by walking, the habit of running by running. If you would be a good reader, read; if a writer, write. But when you shall not have read for thirty days in succession, but have done something else, you will know the consequence. In the same way, if you shall have lain down ten days, get up and attempt to make a long walk, and you will see how your legs are weakened. Generally then if you would make anything a habit, do it; if you would not make it a habit, do not do it, but accustom yourself to do something else in place of it. So it is with respect to the affections of the soul: when you have been angry, you must know that not only has this evil befallen you, but that you have also increased the habit, and in a manner thrown fuel upon fire.

EPICTETUS, *THE TEACHINGS OF A STOIC: SELECTED DISCOURSES AND THE ENCHIRIDION*, "HOW WE SHOULD STRUGGLE AGAINST APPEARANCES" (FROM C. EARLY 2ND CENTURY CE)

ACCEPTANCE

But when set in the very midst of troubles one should say: Perchance some day the memory of this sorrow will even bring delight. Let such a man fight against them with all his might: if he once gives way, he will be vanquished; but if he strives against his sufferings, he will conquer.

LUCIUS SENECA, *LETTERS FROM A STOIC,* "LXXVIII. ON THE HEALING POWER OF THE MIND" (FROM C. 63-65 CE)

VIRTUE

…it is thus that we should live – as if we lived in plain sight of all men; and it is thus that we should think – as if there were someone who could look into our inmost souls; and there is one who can so look. For what avails it that something is hidden from man? Nothing is shut off from the sight of God. He is witness of our souls, and he comes into the very midst of our thoughts – comes into them, I say, as one who may at any time depart.

LUCIUS SENECA, *LETTERS FROM A STOIC,* "XXXIII. ON DRUNKENNESS" (FROM C. 63-65 CE)

GOODNESS

Has then God given you eyes to no purpose? And to no purpose has he infused into them a spirit so strong and of such skilful contrivance as to reach a long way and to fashion the forms of things which are seen? What messenger is so swift and vigilant? … And to no purpose has he made light, without the presence of which there would be no use in any other thing? Man, be neither ungrateful for these gifts nor yet forget the things which are superior to them.

EPICTETUS, *THE TEACHINGS OF A STOIC: SELECTED DISCOURSES AND THE ENCHIRIDION*, "ON THE POWER OF SPEAKING" (FROM C. EARLY 2ND CENTURY CE)

NOBILITY OF THOUGHT

Hence you see why "liberal studies" are so called; it is because they are studies worthy of a free-born gentleman. But there is only one really liberal study – that which gives a man his liberty. It is the study of wisdom, and that is lofty, brave, and great-souled.

LUCIUS SENECA, *LETTERS FROM A STOIC*, "LXXXVIII. ON LIBERAL AND VOCATIONAL STUDIES" (FROM C. 63-65 CE)

WISDOM

329

The beginning of philosophy, to him at least who enters on it in the right way and by the door, is a consciousness of his own weakness and inability about necessary things; for we come into the world with no natural notion of a right-angled triangle, or of a diesis (a quarter tone), or of a half-tone; but we learn each of these things by a certain transmission according to art; and for this reason those who do not know them do not think that they know them. But as to good and evil, and beautiful and ugly, and becoming and unbecoming, and happiness and misfortune, and proper and improper, and what we ought to do and what we ought not to do, who ever came into the world without having an innate idea of them?

EPICTETUS, *THE TEACHINGS OF A STOIC: SELECTED DISCOURSES AND THE ENCHIRIDION,* "WHAT THE BEGINNING OF PHILOSOPHY IS" (FROM C. EARLY 2ND CENTURY CE)

VIRTUE

What do we admire? Externals. About what things are we busy? Externals. And have we any doubt then why we fear or why we are anxious? What then happens when we think the things, which are coming on us, to be evils? It is not in our power not to be afraid, it is not in our power not to be anxious. Then we say, Lord God, how shall I not be anxious? Fool, have you not hands, did not God make them for you? Sit down now and pray that your nose may not run. Wipe yourself rather and do not blame him. Well then, has he given to you nothing in the present case? Has he not given to you endurance? Has he not given to you magnanimity? Has he not given to you manliness? When you have such hands do you still look for one who shall wipe your nose?

EPICTETUS, *THE TEACHINGS OF A STOIC: SELECTED DISCOURSES AND THE ENCHIRIDION*, "THAT WE DO NOT STRIVE TO USE OUR OPINIONS ABOUT GOOD AND EVIL" (FROM C. EARLY 2ND CENTURY CE)

ACCEPTANCE

An expedition will be incomplete if one stops half way, or anywhere on this side of one's destination; but life is not incomplete if it is honourable. At whatever point you leave off living, provided you leave off nobly, your life is a whole. Often, however, one must leave off bravely, and our reasons therefore need not be momentous; for neither are the reasons momentous which hold us here.

LUCIUS SENECA, *LETTERS FROM A STOIC*, "LXXVII. ON TAKING ONE'S OWN LIFE" (FROM C. 63-65 CE)

NOBILITY OF THOUGHT

Take care that thou art not made into a Caesar, that thou art not dyed with this dye; for such things happen. Keep thyself then simple, good, pure, serious, free from affectation, a friend of justice, a worshipper of the gods, kind, affectionate, strenuous in all proper acts. Strive to continue to be such as philosophy wished to make thee. Reverence the gods, and help men. Short is life. There is only one fruit of this terrene life, a pious disposition and social acts.

MARCUS AURELIUS, *MEDITATIONS*, "BOOK VI" (FROM C. 180 CE)

…there is no profit from the things which are valued
and eagerly sought to those who have obtained them;
and to those who have not yet obtained them there is an
imagination, that when these things are come, all that is
good will come with them; then, when they are come,
the feverish feeling is the same, the tossing to and fro is
the same, the satiety, the desire of things, which are not
present; for freedom is acquired not by the full possession of
the things which are desired, but by removing the desire.

EPICTETUS, *THE TEACHINGS OF A STOIC: SELECTED
DISCOURSES AND THE ENCHIRIDION*, "TO THOSE WHO
FALL OFF (DESIST) FROM THEIR PURPOSE"
(FROM C. EARLY 2ND CENTURY CE)

There are times when we ought to die and are unwilling; sometimes we die and are unwilling. No one is so ignorant as not to know that we must at some time die; nevertheless, when one draws near death, one turns to flight, trembles, and laments. Would you not think him an utter fool who wept because he was not alive a thousand years ago? And is he not just as much of a fool who weeps because he will not be alive a thousand years from now? It is all the same; you will not be, and you were not. Neither of these periods of time belongs to you. You have been cast upon this point of time; if you would make it longer, how much longer shall you make it? Why weep? Why pray? You are taking pains to no purpose.

LUCIUS SENECA, *LETTERS FROM A STOIC*, "LXXVII. ON TAKING ONE'S OWN LIFE" (FROM C. 63-65 CE)

WILL

If then I am there where my will is, then only shall I be a friend such as I ought to be, and son, and father; for this will be my interest, to maintain the character of fidelity, of modesty, of patience, of abstinence, of active cooperation, of observing my relations (towards all). But if I put myself in one place, and honesty in another, then the doctrine of Epicurus becomes strong, which asserts either that there is no honesty or it is that which opinion holds to be honest (virtuous).

EPICTETUS, *THE TEACHINGS OF A STOIC: SELECTED DISCOURSES AND THE ENCHIRIDION*, "ON FRIENDSHIP" (FROM C. EARLY 2ND CENTURY CE)

ACCEPTANCE

Remember that in life you ought to behave as at a banquet. Suppose that something is carried round and is opposite to you. Stretch out your hand and take a portion with decency. Suppose that it passes by you. Do not detain it.

EPICTETUS, *THE TEACHINGS OF A STOIC: SELECTED DISCOURSES AND THE ENCHIRIDION*, "THE MANUAL: XV" (FROM C. EARLY 2ND CENTURY CE)

These decrees are unalterable and fixed; they are governed by a mighty and everlasting compulsion. Your goal will be the goal of all things. What is there strange in this to you? You were born to be subject to this law; this fate befell your father, your mother, your ancestors, all who came before you; and it will befall all who shall come after you. A sequence which cannot be broken or altered by any power binds all things together and draws all things in its course. Think of the multitudes of men doomed to death who will come after you, of the multitudes who will go with you! You would die more bravely, I suppose, in the company of many thousands; and yet there are many thousands, both of men and of animals, who at this very moment, while you are irresolute about death, are breathing their last, in their several ways. But you – did you believe that you would not some day reach the goal towards which you have always been travelling? No journey but has its end.

LUCIUS SENECA, *LETTERS FROM A STOIC*, "LXXVII. ON TAKING ONE'S OWN LIFE" (FROM C. 63-65 CE)

VIRTUE

Certain persons have made up their minds that the point at issue with regard to the liberal studies is whether they make men good; but they do not even profess or aim at a knowledge of this particular subject… But which of these paves the way to virtue? Pronouncing syllables, investigating words, memorizing plays, or making rules for the scansion of poetry, what is there in all this that rids one of fear, roots out desire, or bridles the passions? The question is: do such men teach virtue, or not? If they do not teach it, then neither do they transmit it. If they do teach it, they are philosophers. Would you like to know how it happens that they have not taken the chair for the purpose of teaching virtue? See how unlike their subjects are; and yet their subjects would resemble each other if they taught the same thing.

LUCIUS SENECA, *LETTERS FROM A STOIC*, "LXXXVIII. ON LIBERAL AND VOCATIONAL STUDIES" (FROM C. 63-65 CE)

VIRTUE

339

For when you have once desired money, if reason be applied to lead to a perception of the evil, the desire is stopped, and the ruling faculty of our mind is restored to the original authority. But if you apply no means of cure, it no longer returns to the same state, but being again excited by the corresponding appearance, it is inflamed to desire quicker than before: and when this takes place continually, it is henceforth hardened (made callous), and the disease of the mind confirms the love of money.

EPICTETUS, *THE TEACHINGS OF A STOIC: SELECTED DISCOURSES AND THE ENCHIRIDION*, "HOW WE SHOULD STRUGGLE AGAINST APPEARANCES" (FROM C. EARLY 2ND CENTURY CE)

TIME

340

Death, however, should be looked in the face by young and old alike. We are not summoned according to our rating on the censor's list. Moreover, no one is so old that it would be improper for him to hope for another day of existence. And one day, mind you, is a stage on life's journey.

LUCIUS SENECA, *LETTERS FROM A STOIC*, "XII. ON OLD AGE" (FROM C. 63-65 CE)

VIRTUE

341

One thing here is worth a great deal, to pass thy life in truth and justice, with a benevolent disposition even to liars and unjust men. When thou wishest to delight thyself, think of the virtues of those who live with thee; for instance, the activity of one, and the modesty of another, and the liberality of a third, and some other good quality of a fourth.

MARCUS AURELIUS, *MEDITATIONS*, "BOOK VI" (FROM C. 180 CE)

GOODNESS

342

My friends, too, helped me greatly toward good health; I used to be comforted by their cheering words, by the hours they spent at my bedside, and by their conversation. Nothing, my excellent Lucilius, refreshes and aids a sick man so much as the affection of his friends; nothing so steals away the expectation and the fear of death. In fact, I could not believe that, if they survived me, I should be dying at all. Yes, I repeat, it seemed to me that I should continue to live, not with them, but through them. I imagined myself not to be yielding up my soul, but to be making it over to them.

LUCIUS SENECA, *LETTERS FROM A STOIC*, "LXXVIII. ON THE HEALING POWER OF THE MIND" (FROM C. 63-65 CE)

GOODNESS

For nature does not bestow virtue; it is an art to become good... Virtue is not vouchsafed to a soul unless that soul has been trained and taught, and by instruction, there is but the stuff of virtue, not virtue itself.

LUCIUS SENECA, *LETTERS FROM A STOIC*, "XC. ON THE PART PLAYED BY PHILOSOPHY IN THE PROGRESS OF MAN" (FROM C. 63-65 CE)

VIRTUE

On the occasion of every accident (event) that befalls you, remember to turn to yourself and inquire what power you have for turning it to use. If you see a fair man or a fair woman, you will find that the power to resist is temperance (continence). If labour (pain) be presented to you, you will find that it is endurance. If it be abusive words, you will find it to be patience. And if you have been thus formed to the (proper) habit, the appearances will not carry you along with them.

EPICTETUS, *THE TEACHINGS OF A STOIC: SELECTED DISCOURSES AND THE ENCHIRIDION*, "THE MANUAL: X" (FROM C. EARLY 2ND CENTURY CE)

Every variety of pain has its premonitory symptoms; this is true, at any rate, of pain that is habitual and recurrent. One can endure the suffering which disease entails, if one has come to regard its results with scorn. But do not of your own accord make your troubles heavier to bear and burden yourself with complaining. Pain is slight if opinion has added nothing to it; but if, on the other hand, you begin to encourage yourself and say, "It is nothing – a trifling matter at most; keep a stout heart and it will soon cease"; then in thinking it slight, you will make it slight. Everything depends on opinion; ambition, luxury, greed, hark back to opinion. It is according to opinion that we suffer. A man is as wretched as he has convinced himself that he is.

LUCIUS SENECA, *LETTERS FROM A STOIC*, "LXXVIII. ON THE HEALING POWER OF THE MIND" (FROM C. 63-65 CE)

WILL

346

He who loves fame considers another man's activity to be his own good; and he who loves pleasure, his own sensations; but he who has understanding, considers his own acts to be his own good. It is in our power to have no opinion about a thing, and not to be disturbed in our soul; for things themselves have no natural power to form our judgements… No man will hinder thee from living according to the reason of thy own nature: nothing will happen to thee contrary to the reason of the universal nature.

MARCUS AURELIUS, *MEDITATIONS*, "BOOK VI" (FROM C. 180 CE)

GOODNESS

347

I can show you many who have lacked, not a friend, but a friendship; this, however, cannot possibly happen when souls are drawn together by identical inclinations into an alliance of honourable desires. And why can it not happen? Because in such cases men know that they have all things in common, especially their troubles.

LUCIUS SENECA, *LETTERS FROM A STOIC*, "VI. ON SHARING KNOWLEDGE" (FROM C. 63-65 CE)

NOBILITY OF THOUGHT

To whom then does the contemplation of these matters (philosophical inquiries) belong? To him who has leisure, for man is an animal that loves contemplation.

EPICTETUS, *THE TEACHINGS OF A STOIC: SELECTED DISCOURSES AND THE ENCHIRIDION*, "ON CONSTANCY (OR FIRMNESS)" (FROM C. EARLY 2ND CENTURY CE)

TIME

What benefit is there in reviewing past sufferings, and in being unhappy, just because once you were unhappy? Besides, every one adds much to his own ills, and tells lies to himself. And that which was bitter to bear is pleasant to have borne; it is natural to rejoice at the ending of one's ills. Two elements must therefore be rooted out once and for all – the fear of future suffering, and the recollection of past suffering; since the latter no longer concerns me, and the former concerns me not yet.

LUCIUS SENECA, *LETTERS FROM A STOIC*, "LXXVIII. ON THE HEALING POWER OF THE MIND" (FROM C. 63-65 CE)

When you see a person weeping in sorrow either when a child goes abroad or when he is dead, or when the man has lost his property, take care that the appearance do not hurry you away with it, as if he were suffering in external things. But straightway make a distinction in your own mind, and be in readiness to say, it is not that which has happened that afflicts this man, for it does not afflict another, but it is the opinion about this thing which afflicts the man. So far as words then do not be unwilling to show him sympathy, and even if it happens so, to lament with him. But take care that you do not lament internally also.

EPICTETUS, *THE TEACHINGS OF A STOIC: SELECTED DISCOURSES AND THE ENCHIRIDION*, "THE MANUAL: XVI" (FROM C. EARLY 2ND CENTURY CE)

TIME

351

If any god told thee that thou shalt die tomorrow,
or certainly on the day after tomorrow, thou wouldst
not care much whether it was on the third day or on
the morrow, unless thou wast in the highest degree
mean-spirited – for how small is the difference?
So think it no great thing to die after as many years
as thou canst name rather than tomorrow.

MARCUS AURELIUS, *MEDITATIONS*, "BOOK IV"
(FROM C. 180 CE)

DETACHMENT

352

Thus, whatever phase of things human and divine you
have apprehended, you will be wearied by the vast number
of things to be answered and things to be learned. And in
order that these manifold and mighty subjects may have free
entertainment in your soul, you must remove there from all
superfluous things.

LUCIUS SENECA, *LETTERS FROM A STOIC*, "LXXXVIII. ON
LIBERAL ARTS AND VOCATIONAL STUDIES" (FROM C. 63-65 CE)

For he who has had a fever, and has been relieved from it, is not in the same state that he was before, unless he has been completely cured. Something of the kind happens also in diseases of the soul. Certain traces and blisters are left in it, and unless a man shall completely efface them, when he is again lashed on the same places, the lash will produce not blisters (weals) but sores. If then you wish not to be of an angry temper, do not feed the habit: throw nothing on it which will increase it: at first keep quiet, and count the days on which you have not been angry. I used to be in passion every day; now every second day; then every third, then every fourth. But if you have intermitted thirty days, make a sacrifice to God. For the habit at first begins to be weakened, and then is completely destroyed... Be willing at length to be approved by yourself, be willing to appear beautiful to God, desire to be in purity with your own pure self and with God.

EPICTETUS, *THE TEACHINGS OF A STOIC: SELECTED DISCOURSES AND THE ENCHIRIDION*, "HOW WE SHOULD STRUGGLE AGAINST APPEARANCES" (FROM C. EARLY 2ND CENTURY CE)

Things themselves (materials) are indifferent; but the use of them is not indifferent. How then shall a man preserve firmness and tranquillity, and at the same time be careful and neither rash nor negligent? If he imitates those who play at dice. The counters are indifferent; the dice are indifferent. How do I know what the cast will be? But to use carefully and dexterously the cast of the dice, this is my business. Thus then in life also the chief business is this: distinguish and separate things, and say: Externals are not in my power: will is in my power. Where shall I seek the good and the bad? Within, in the things which are my own. But in what does not belong to you call nothing either good or bad, or profit or damage or anything of the kind.

EPICTETUS, *THE TEACHINGS OF A STOIC: SELECTED DISCOURSES AND THE ENCHIRIDION*, "HOW MAGNANIMITY IS CONSISTENT WITH CARE" (FROM C. EARLY 2ND CENTURY CE)

TIME

355

Surely you are aware that dying is also one of life's duties?
You are deserting no duty; for there is no definite number
established which you are bound to complete. There is
no life that is not short.

LUCIUS SENECA, *LETTERS FROM A STOIC*, "LXXVII.
ON TAKING ONE'S OWN LIFE" AND "FRIENDSHIP"
(FROM C. 63-65 CE)

WILL

356

…if you wish to prove that a good man ought not to get
drunk, why work it out by logic? Show how base it is to pour
down more liquor than one can carry, and not to know the
capacity of one's own stomach; show how often the drunkard
does things which make him blush when he is sober; state that
drunkenness is nothing but a condition of insanity purposely
assumed. Prolong the drunkard's condition to several days;
will you have any doubt about his madness? Even as it is,
the madness is no less; it merely lasts a shorter time.

LUCIUS SENECA, *LETTERS FROM A STOIC*, "LXXIX.
ON DRUNKENNESS" (FROM C. 63-65 CE)

COOPERATION WITH NATURE

Dost thou not see the little plants, the little birds, the ants, the spiders, the bees working together to put in order their several parts of the universe? And art thou unwilling to do the work of a human being, and dost thou not make haste to do that which is according to thy nature? But it is necessary to take rest also. It is necessary: however nature has fixed bounds to this too: she has fixed bounds both to eating and drinking, and yet thou goest beyond these bounds, beyond what is sufficient; yet in thy acts it is not so, but thou stoppest short of what thou canst do. So thou lovest not thyself, for if thou didst, thou wouldst love thy nature and her will.

MARCUS AURELIUS, *MEDITATIONS*, "BOOK V" (FROM C. 180 CE)

NOBILITY OF THOUGHT

How much trouble he avoids who does not look to see what his neighbour says or does or thinks, but only to what he does himself, that it may be just and pure; or as Agathon says, look not round at the depraved morals of others, but run straight along the line without deviating from it.

MARCUS AURELIUS, *MEDITATIONS*, "BOOK IV" (FROM C. 180 CE)

WILL

Thus we also act: in what cases do we fear? In things which are independent of the will. In what cases on the contrary do we behave with confidence, as if there were no danger? In things dependent on the will. To be deceived then, or to act rashly, or shamelessly, or with base desire to seek something, does not concern us at all, if we only hit the mark in things which are independent of our will. But where there is death or exile or pain or infamy, there we attempt to run away, there we are struck with terror. Therefore, as we may expect it to happen with those who err in the greatest matters, we convert natural confidence (that is, according to nature) into audacity, desperation, rashness, shamelessness; and we convert natural caution and modesty into cowardice and meanness, which are full of fear and confusion.

EPICTETUS, *THE TEACHINGS OF A STOIC: SELECTED DISCOURSES AND THE ENCHIRIDION*, "THAT CONFIDENCE (COURAGE) IS NOT INCONSISTENT WITH CAUTION" (FROM C. EARLY 2ND CENTURY CE)

ACCEPTANCE

All these things, however, can be easily endured – gruel, warm water, and anything else that seems insupportable to a fastidious man, to one who is wallowing in luxury, sick in soul rather than in body – if only we cease to shudder at death. And we shall cease, if once we have gained a knowledge of the limits of good and evil; then, and then only, life will not weary us, neither will death make us afraid.

LUCIUS SENECA, *LETTERS FROM A STOIC*, "LXXVIII. ON THE HEALING POWER OF THE MIND" (FROM C. 63-65 CE)

GOODNESS

The perfection of moral character consists in this, in passing every day as the last, and in being neither violently excited nor torpid nor playing the hypocrite… But thou, who art destined to end so soon, art thou wearied of enduring the bad, and this too when thou art one of them? It is a ridiculous thing for a man not to fly from his own badness, which is indeed possible, but to fly from other men's badness, which is impossible.

MARCUS AURELIUS, *MEDITATIONS*, "BOOK VII" (FROM C. 180 CE)

DETACHMENT

362

…we ought not to desire in every way what is not our own. And the sorrow of another is another's sorrow; but my sorrow is my own. I then will stop my own sorrow by every means, for it is in my power; and the sorrow of another I will endeavour to stop as far as I can; but I will not attempt to do it by every means; for if I do, I shall be fighting against God…

EPICTETUS, *THE TEACHINGS OF A STOIC: SELECTED DISCOURSES AND THE ENCHIRIDION*, "THE MANUAL: L" (FROM C. EARLY 2ND CENTURY CE)

VIRTUE

363

Remember that it is not he who reviles you or strikes you, who insults you, but it is your opinion about these things as being insulting. When then a man irritates you, you must know that it is your own opinion which has irritated you.

EPICTETUS, *THE TEACHINGS OF A STOIC: SELECTED DISCOURSES AND THE ENCHIRIDION*, "THE MANUAL: XX" (FROM C. EARLY 2ND CENTURY CE)

WISDOM

364

I disagree with those who strike out into the midst of the billows and, welcoming a stormy existence, wrestle daily in hardihood of soul with life's problems. The wise man will endure all that, but will not choose it; he will prefer to be at peace rather than at war. It helps little to have cast out your own faults if you must quarrel with those of others.

LUCIUS SENECA, *LETTERS FROM A STOIC*, "XXVIII. ON TRAVEL AS A CURE FOR DISCONTENT" (FROM C. 63-65 CE)

WILL

365

It is your body that is hampered by ill-health, and not your soul as well. It is for this reason that it clogs the feet of the runner… but if your soul be habitually in practice, you will plead and teach, listen and learn, investigate and meditate. What more is necessary? Do you think that you are doing nothing if you possess self-control in your illness? You will be showing that a disease can be overcome, or at any rate endured.

LUCIUS SENECA, *LETTERS FROM A STOIC*, "LXXVIII. ON THE HEALING POWER OF THE MIND" (FROM C. 63-65 CE)

INDEX BY THEME

INDEX BY STOIC

FURTHER READING

All the quotes in this book were sourced from the following original texts:

Meditations, Marcus Aurelius
(Collins Classics, 2020)

Letters from a Stoic, Lucius Seneca
(Collins Classics, 2020)

The Teachings of a Stoic: Selected Discourses and the Encheiridion, Epictetus
(Collins Classics, 2023)

ACKNOWLEDGEMENTS

When I was asked to create this little book I nearly jumped out of my skin with non-Stoical exuberance. This project gave me the excuse to spend a significant amount of my time with three very fine minds who perplexed and challenged me for weeks on end. As I predicted (and hoped), this book project became the most cathartic one I have taken on thus far, and I honestly don't know how I got through life before absorbing this perennial Stoic wisdom.

A hearty thanks to my ever encouraging, resilient and enthusiastic editor, Simon Holland, who made a very tight deadline seem more like a fun challenge than a headache!